THE
EXCELLENT

History of the Mer-
chant of *Venice*.

With the extreme cruelty of *Shylocke*
the Iew towards the saide Merchant, in cutting a iust pound of his flesh. And the obtaining
of *Portia*, by the choyse of
three Caskets.

Written by W. SHAKESPEARE.

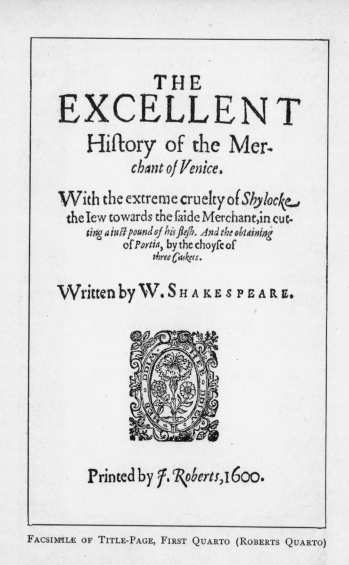

Printed by *J. Roberts*, 1600.

THE NEW HUDSON SHAKESPEARE

THE MERCHANT OF VENICE

INTRODUCTION AND NOTES BY

HENRY NORMAN HUDSON, LL·D·

EDITED AND REVISED BY

EBENEZER CHARLTON BLACK LL·D· (GLASGOW)

WITH THE COÖPERATION OF

ANDREW JACKSON GEORGE L·LIT·D· (AMHERST)

GINN AND COMPANY
BOSTON NEW YORK CHICAGO LONDON
ATLANTA DALLAS COLUMBUS SAN FRANCISCO

The Athenæum Press
GINN AND COMPANY · PRO-
PRIETORS · BOSTON · U.S.A.

PREFACE

The text of this edition of *The Merchant of Venice* is based upon a collation of the Quartos of 1600 and the seventeenth century Folios. Exclusive of changes in spelling, punctuation, and stage directions, only five emendations by eighteenth century and nineteenth century editors have been incorporated into the text; and these, with every variation from the First Folio, are indicated in the textual notes. The only omissions are such passages as are out of place in a school edition.

The spelling and the punctuation of the text are modern, except in the case of verb terminations in *-ed*, which, when the *e* is silent, are printed with the apostrophe in its place. This is the general usage in the First Folio. Modern spelling has to a certain extent been followed in the text variants; but the original spelling has been retained wherever its peculiarities have been the basis for important textual criticism and emendation.

With regard to the general plan of this revision of Hudson's Shakespeare, Professor W. P. Trent, of Columbia University, has offered valuable suggestions and given important advice.

August 14, 1906

CONTENTS

INTRODUCTION

vi CONTENTS

THE TEXT

INTRODUCTION

NOTE. In citations from Shakespeare's plays and nondramatic poems the numbering has reference to the Globe edition, except in the case of this play, where the reference is to this edition.

I. SOURCES

The Merchant of Venice is woven out of story-threads as old and as varied as human nature. Four distinct sets of these story-threads, two primary — the Caskets and the Pound of Flesh (or the Bond) — and two secondary — Jessica's Elopement and the Rings — are in the web of the complete plot. They may be regarded as subplots, and in this summary of sources will naturally be considered first, and in the order in which they come into the play.

THE SUBPLOTS

1. *The Caskets.* The device of the caskets, varied occasionally by the substitution of vats, or even of cakes and of pasties, for chests and coffers, is found in many languages and is probably of oriental origin. The underlying philosophy of choice as the foundation of moral activity may be read in the *Genesis* narrative of the fall of man and in the mythologies of all Indo-European peoples. In mediæval literature the caskets-form of the story takes definite shape in the Greek romance, *Barlaam and Josaphat*, by Joannes

Damascenus (*circa* 800) [1]; and through a Latin translation in the *Speculum Historiale* of Vincent de Beauvais it made its way into *The Golden Legend* of Jacobus de Voragine. In Boccaccio's *Decameron* and in Gower's *Confessio Amantis* are interesting variants. The popular collection of stories in Latin called the *Gesta Romanorum*, compiled about the year 1300, contains the version most similar to that in *The Merchant of Venice;* and it is significant that this version is found in the English translation of the *Gesta* printed by Wynkin de Worde — a translation so popular in Elizabethan England as to be issued six times between 1577 and 1601 under the title *Records of Ancyent Historyes.*

2. *The Pound of Flesh (or the Bond).* In the *Mahábhárata*, in Aryan myth and folk-tale generally, and in Egyptian and oriental literatures, may be read the germ-ideas of the bond story. Like that of the caskets, it has its foundations deep in man's moral nature. In essence, it is the *lex talionis* in its relation to the Christian principle of mercy and forgiveness. It is significant that the first specific reference in English literature to the flesh-without-blood incident is in the *Cursor Mundi (circa* 1320), a Northumbrian religious poem which curiously anticipates later fourteenth century miracle-play cycles. In this poem a Jew guides the Empress Helena to the place where the true cross is concealed, and reveals the secret to save himself from punishment for having tried to enforce his terrible flesh compact with a Christian. The mediæval conception of Christ's sacrifice, and the popular interpretation of the terrible Roman law of the

[1] Translations, transcripts, or summaries of all the more important source-versions will be found in the Appendix of Furness's *A New Variorum Edition — The Merchant of Venice.*

Twelve Tables which gave a creditor full power over the person of a debtor, are responsible for the dozen and more versions of the bond story (with, or without, a Jew; sometimes with *The Merchant of Venice* positions of Jew and Christian reversed) which were current in Europe in short story collections — *Gesta Romanorum, Dolopathos*, etc. — between 1400 and 1600. In one version the compact turns upon the right to gouge out one of the creditor's eyes — a punishment inflicted oftener upon Jews than by them, and one that may be grimly suggested in *The Merchant of Venice*, II, v, 42. Important among these many versions is the ninety-fifth "declamation" in *The Orator . . . Written in French by Alexander Silvayn and Englished by L. P.*,[1] *London . . . 1596:* "Of a Jew who would for his debt have a pound of the flesh of a Christian." Shylock's speeches in the trial scene strongly resemble the arguments of the Jew in this 'declamation.' Important, too, is the version of the story in the ballad, *Gernutus the Jew*, preserved in the Pepysian Library, Magdalene College, Cambridge, and printed somewhat carelessly in Percy's *Reliques:* "A new Song, shewing the crueltie of Gernutus, a Jewe, who lending to a merchant an hundred crownes, would have a pound of his fleshe, because he could not pay him at the time appointed. . . ." There is uncertainty as to the date of this ballad, but the weight of evidence is in favor of its antedating Shakespeare's play. Of all the possible source-versions of the bond story, the closest in resemblance to *The Merchant of Venice* is in Ser Giovanni Fiorentino's [2] collection of romances, *Il Pecorone*, written, as we are quaintly

---

[1] That is, Lazarus Piot, a *nom de guerre* of Anthony Munday.

[2] Probably an assumed name.

told, three years after the death of Boccaccio. In *Il Pecorone* is introduced a lady of 'Belmonte'; the usurer is a Jew of Mestre, near Venice; and the flesh-without-the-blood argument is used by a woman disguised as a lawyer.

3. *Jessica's Elopement.* This story has been traced to the fourteenth *novellino* of Masuccio di Salerno, which tells how the daughter of a rich miser of Naples stole her father's jewels and eloped with her lover. But the theme is common to the fiction, prose and verse, of many countries.

4. *The Rings.* This episode is found in *Il Pecorone*.

The Main Plot

That the ancient stories of the caskets and the pound of flesh were combined in a drama before Shakespeare wrote *The Merchant of Venice*, is clear from what Stephen Gosson says in *The Schoole of Abuse*, published in 1579. He makes distinct reference to a play, now lost, called *The Jew*, ". . . representing the greedinesse of worldly chusers, and bloody mindes of Usurers. . . ." Under the date August 25, 1594, Henslowe in his *Diary* mentions as a new play *the Venesyon comodey* (The Venetian Comedy) which Fleay claims as a lost work of Dekker's, *The Jew of Venice*, upon which he asserts that Shakespeare's play was based. Sidney Lee suggests that *the Venesyon comodey* was Shakespeare's revision of some old play made when popular interest in things Jewish was at fever heat over the trial in February, 1594, and the execution in the following June, of Queen Elizabeth's Jewish physician, Roderigo Lopez. It is interesting to note that the chief undoer of Lopez was Antonio Perez, usually called Don Antonio. "That a Christian named Antonio should be the cause of the ruin alike of the greatest Jew in Elizabethan England and of the greatest Jew of the Elizabethan drama, is a curious confirmation of the theory that Lopez was the begetter of Shylock"—Lee. In the play, *The Three Ladies of London*, by R. W. (1584), a Jewish creditor, Gerontus — evidently the same name as that of the Jew in the ballad mentioned above — tries to recover a loan of three thousand ducats for three months from a Christian debtor, Mercatore.

The influence of Marlowe's *The Jew of Malta* makes itself felt in general inspiration rather than in plan and details of plot, though Abigail's attitude to her father, Barabas, and her leaving him through love of a Christian, strongly suggest the relations between Jessica, Shylock, and Lorenzo.

•

II. DATE OF COMPOSITION

The only thing certain about the date of composition of *The Merchant of Venice* is that it was written before 1598. In that year we have two independent references to it: (1) in the *Palladis Tamia, Wits Treasury; being the Second Part of Wits Commonwealth* of Francis Meres; and (2) in *The Stationers' Registers*. It is sixth in the list of twelve Shakespeare plays, and last of the six comedies, mentioned in the *Palladis Tamia*, that famous *terminus ante quem* in Shakespeare chronology, the largest bit of solid rock amid the shifting sands of conjecture as to date of composition. Under the date July 22, 1598, James Roberts (the name is spelled here and elsewhere, Robertes) had the play entered in *The Stationers' Registers* under the title "a booke of the Marchaunt of Venyce or otherwise called the

Jewe of Venyce," with the significant proviso that " yt bee not prynted by the said James Robertes or anye other what-soeuer without lycence first had from the Right honourable the lord Chamberlen." At that time the theatrical company to which Shakespeare belonged bore the title of "The Lord Chamberlain's Servants," and the proviso indicates suspicion of Roberts, the probability that his copy was "stolen and surreptitious,"[1] and a desire to keep the play out of print until the company gave official sanction through its patron. This sanction seems to have been granted within two years, for in 1600 two editions of the play were published.

Attempts have been made to give an approximate date to the composition by identifying it with one or other of the plays discussed in the preceding section, notably *the Venesyon comodey*, but the theories advanced are only inter-esting guesses. A judicious application of the leading inter-nal tests would indicate that the date of composition was as near as possible to the *terminus ante quem*.[2] Every-where the play shows the easy freedom of conscious mastery, the characters being so entirely under the author's control, and subdued to his hand, that he seems to let them talk and act just as they have a mind to. The style throughout is so

---

[1] " . . . You were abus'd with diuerse stolne and surreptitious copies, maimed and deformed by the frauds and stealthes of iniuri-ous impostors" (Heminge and Condell's address "To the Great Variety of Readers," First Folio, 1623).

[2] But Conrad, in his *Metrische Untersuchungen*, *Shakespeare Jahrbuch*, XXXI, 326, bases a plea for 1595 upon an analysis of verse structure. On the other hand, Ward, in the new and revised edition (1899) of his *History of English Dramatic Literature*, tends away from the early date to which he was inclined when the first edition of his work was published.

even and sustained, the word and the character are so fitted to each other, the laws of dramatic proportion are so well observed, and the work is so free from any jarring or falling out from the due course and order of art, as to justify the conclusion accepted by several recent editors that the play was written at such a stage of intellectual growth and furnishing as Shakespeare undoubtedly had reached by the beginning of the year 1598.

III. EDITIONS

QUARTOS

Two Quarto editions of *The Merchant of Venice* were published in the year 1600 :

(1) A sixpenny Quarto of forty leaves, with the title-page which is shown in facsimile in the frontispiece of this volume.

As this — sometimes called the Roberts Quarto — was evidently the first of the two 1600 Quartos to be entered on *The Stationers' Registers* (see above), though its priority of publication is uncertain, J. P. Kemble (1798) called it the First Quarto ; and this nomenclature has been adopted by the editors of the Cambridge Shakespeare and by almost all the leading Shakespeare scholars and editors of recent years. In this edition it is designated Q_1.

(2) A Quarto of 38 leaves, with the title-page shown in facsimile on the following page.

This — sometimes known as the Heyes[1] Quarto — is called by the Cambridge editors the Second Quarto, though

---

[1] In *The Stationers' Registers*, under the date " 28 Octobris (1600, 42 Regine)," when this Quarto seems to have been entered, the name is given as " Thomas haies."

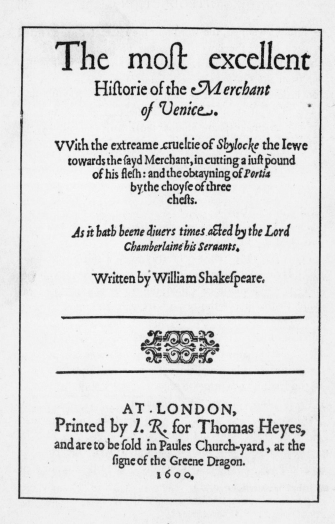

The moſt excellent

Hiſtorie of the *Merchant*
of *Venice*.

VVith the extreame crueltie of *Shylocke* the Iewe
towards the ſayd Merchant, in cutting a iuſt pound
of his fleſh: and the obtayning of *Portia*
by the choyſe of three
cheſts.

As it hath beene diuers times acted by the Lord
Chamberlaine his Seruants.

Written by William Shakeſpeare.

AT . LONDON,
Printed by *I. R.* for Thomas Heyes,
and are to be ſold in Paules Church-yard, at the
ſigne of the Greene Dragon.
1 6 0 0.

Johnson and Capell, believing in its priority, named it the
First Quarto. In this edition it is designated Q_2.

Each of these Quartos — the only editions of the play
that are known to have appeared in Shakespeare's lifetime
— seems to have been printed from a different transcript of
what was probably the author's original copy, that of Q_1
being the work of a careful copyist, that of Q_2 of one more
careless if not more illiterate.

In 1637 Laurence Hayes (Heyes, Haies), son of the pub-
lisher of Q_2, published what is now known as the Third Quarto
(Q_3), having entered it on *The Stationers' Registers* eighteen
years before (Regni Regis 17° 8° Julii, 1619). Q_3 is in the
main but a careless reprint of Q_2, but in it appears "The
Actors Names" — the first list of dramatis personæ.

In 1652 appeared the Fourth Quarto (Q_4), which seems
but a reissue of Q_3 with a new title-page. ". . . It is
undoubtedly a fact worth remarking, — that just at the time
of this reissue the Jews were beginning to ask for readmis-
sion into England, and the consideration of their request to
be seriously entertained." — Hales.

FOLIOS

In the First Folio (1623), designated in this edition F_1,
the text of *The Merchant of Venice* is very similar to that
of Q_2, but here for the first time is found the formal division into acts. The Second Folio, F_2 (1632), the Third
Folio, F_3 (1663, 1664), and the Fourth Folio, F_4 (1685),
show few real variants in the text of this play and none
of great importance.

ROWE'S EDITIONS

In 1709 Nicholas Rowe, poet laureate from 1715 to 1718, published what is the first critical and the first octavo edition of Shakespeare and issued a second and enlarged edition five years later. Rowe, himself a practical playwright, made the excellent division of acts into scenes which almost all later editors have accepted ; and he introduced the list of dramatis personæ which has been made the basis for all later lists.

IV. DRAMATIC STRUCTURE AND MANAGEMENT OF TIME AND PLACE

The essential elements of a drama are (1) the exposition or introduction, (2) the complication or rising action, (3) the climax or turning point, (4) the resolution or falling action, and (5) the catastrophe or conclusion. In a tragic drama the hero struggles with antagonizing forces and is defeated ; in comedy he triumphs. *The Merchant of Venice* is a comedy in which Antonio triumphs over the difficulties and complications woven around him in the rising action. Here as in Shakespeare's other plays the organic parts of the action do not correspond exactly to the mechanical division into acts. In this play the exposition is contained in the first two scenes ; the complication begins with the conversation between Bassanio and Shylock regarding the loan, and continues until the climax is reached in the casket scene of the third act, at the close of which is read Antonio's letter to Bassanio announcing the desperate condition of his affairs. The beginning of the resolution is usually in the closest union with the climax, and Portia's sending Bassanio to the relief of Antonio is incorporated with the casket scene. The resolution or falling action is complete with the close of the trial scene and the episode of the rings. This episode, linking the tragic subaction to the comic main action, brings about the exquisite conclusion amid the music and the moonlight of Belmont.

The Merchant of Venice is a romantic drama in which the classical unities of time and place are quietly set aside in favor of the supreme unity of life. In the action of the play a quarter of a year is made to pass, and, as we read or listen, it seems a matter of a few hours. The scene shifts from Venice to Belmont and from Belmont to Venice ; and such improbabilities as the stories of the bond and of the caskets are interwoven with Jessica's elopement and the episode of the rings into a symmetrical, fascinating, and convincing plot. Eccles[1] has one formal time analysis ; Halpin, another ; P. A. Daniel, a third. Christopher North (Professor John Wilson) published in *Blackwood's Edinburgh Magazine* a theory of 'double time,' as used by Shakespeare : "Shakespeare counts off days and hours, as it were, by two clocks, on one of which the true Historic time is recorded, and on the other the Dramatic time, or a false show of time, whereby days, weeks, and months may be to the utmost contracted." But such ingenious theories and analyses are beside the mark when the difference between a poet's point of view and a scientist's is recognized. Shakespeare's time, like Sir Walter Scott's, is independent

[1] See Furness's *A New Variorum Edition — The Merchant of Venice,* "The Duration of the Action," 332–341.

of chronometers and almanacs; and in his treatment of localities it is but a fool's errand to go for help to the maps and charts of the formal geographer.

V. VERSIFICATION AND DICTION

BLANK VERSE

The greater part of *The Merchant of Venice* is in blank verse [1] — the rhymeless, iambic five-stress verse (iambic pentameter) introduced into England from Italy by Henry Howard, Earl of Surrey, about 1540, and used by him in a translation of the second and fourth books of Vergil's *Æneid*. Nicholas Grimald (*Tottel's Miscellany*, 1557) employed the measure for the first time in English original poetry, and its roots began to strike deep into British soil and absorb substance. It is peculiarly significant that Sackville and Norton should have used it as the measure of *Gorboduc*, the first English tragedy (performed by "the Gentlemen of the Inner Temple" on January 18, 1561, and first printed in 1565). About the time when Shakespeare arrived in London the infinite possibilities of blank verse as a vehicle for dramatic poetry and passion were being shown by Kyd and above all by Marlowe. The blank verse of Shakespeare's earlier plays, like that of Surrey and Sackville, is for the most part restrained and monotonously regular; in his later plays it breaks away from the formal verse limits and sweeps all before it in its freedom, power,

---

[1] The term 'blank verse' is used for the first time in Nash's Preface to Greene's *Menaphon* (1589), where we find the expression: "the swelling bumbast of bragging blanke verse."

and organic continuity. In the blank verse of *The Merchant of Venice* we have the transition from the earlier style to the later, and trochees, spondees, feminine endings, run-on lines, incomplete lines, Alexandrines, etc., vary the rhythm and give flexibility and vigor, though end-stopped lines abound, many of them (for instance, the first line of the play) examples of normal five-stress iambic pentameter.

Rhyme

When compared with Shakespeare's earlier plays, *The Merchant of Venice* shows a marked decrease in the use of rhyme in the dialogue. With the ever-increasing freedom from metrical restraint which distinguishes Shakespeare's development as a writer of verse, there is less and less employment of rhymed couplets, and in this play, as in the later plays, these couplets are for the most part rhyme-tags at the close of scenes.

The scrolls within the caskets are in four-stress trochaic verse catalectic, varied by normal four-stress iambic lines.

"Tell me where is fancy bred" is the only song in the play, but, woven of trochaic and iambic rhyming lines, it is one of the daintiest in the precious volume of Shakespeare's lyrics that dally "with the innocence of love like the old age."

Prose

In the development of the English drama the use of prose as a vehicle of expression entitled to equal rights with verse, was due to Lyly. He was the first to use prose with power and distinction in original plays, and did memorable service in preparing the way for Shakespeare's achievement as a master of humorous prose in high comedy. In Shakespeare's prose, as has been pointed out by Delius (*Die Prosa in Shakespeares Dramen*, *Shakespeare Jahrbuch*, V, 227–273) three varieties may be distinguished : (1) The speech of the comic characters, clowns, and their fellows, which in phraseology, dialect, and construction is the speech of the common people. Such is what we have in the talk of Launcelot and Old Gobbo. (2) The essentially euphuistic prose, features of which are at times introduced in Shakespeare's earlier plays in order to ridicule it, but occur in his later dramas without any such purpose and in full seriousness where information is to be given as to the nature of a situation, or where a specially solemn and ceremonious tone is intended. (3) The humorous prose spoken as a rule, though not exclusively, by persons of superior rank or importance — the prose of high comedy, vivacious, sparkling, and flashing with repartee. Examples of this are the conversations between Portia and Nerissa in this play and the wit-combats in *Much Ado About Nothing*.

VI. GENERAL CHARACTERISTICS

While *The Merchant of Venice* shows no novelty either of story or of plot, Shakespeare here as elsewhere making use of material common to European and oriental literature and of universal appeal, it is one of the most original productions of the human mind by virtue of conception and development of character, poetical texture and grain, sap and flavor of wit and humor, and all that touches the real life and virtue of workmanship. The praise of the play is in the mouth of all who have vision to discern. From the reopening of the theaters at the Restoration till the present day, it has kept its place on the stage ; it is among the first of Shakespeare's works to be read, and the last to be forgotten ; its interest is as durable in the closet as on the boards.

Critics have too often entertained themselves with speculations as to the specific moral purpose in this play or that. A work of art, to be really deserving the name, must needs be moral, because it must be proportionable and true to nature, thus attuning our inward forces to the voice of external order and law; otherwise it is at strife with the compact of things, a piece of dissonance, a jarring, unbalanced, crazy thing, that will die of its own internal disorder. If, then, a work be morally bad, this proves the author more a bungler than anything else. And if any one admire it or take pleasure in it, he does so, not from reason, but from something within him of which his reason, in so far as he has any, necessarily disapproves : so that he is rather to be laughed at as a dunce than preached to as a sinner.

As to the moral temper of *The Merchant of Venice*, critics have differed widely, some regarding the play as teaching the most comprehensive humanity, others as caressing the narrowest bigotries of the Elizabethan age. This difference may be fairly taken as an argument for Shakespeare's candor and evenhandedness. A special pleader is not apt to leave the hearers in doubt on which side of the question he stands. In this play, as in others, the poet ordered things mainly with a view to dramatic effect, though to such effect in the largest and noblest sense. And the highest praise compatible with tne nature of the work is justly his, inasmuch as he did not allow himself to be swayed either way from the right measures and proportions of art. For art is, from its very nature, obliged to be " without respect of persons." Impartiality is its essential law, the constituent of its being. And of Shakespeare it could least of all be said,—

> he narrow'd his mind,
> And to party gave up what was meant for mankind.

He represented men as he had seen them. And he could neither repeal nor ignore the old law of human nature, in virtue of which the wisest and kindest men are more or less warped by social customs and prejudices, so that they come to do, and even to make a merit of doing, some things that are very unwise and unkind ; while the wrongs and insults which they are thus led to practice have the effect of goading the sufferers into savage malignity and revenge. Had he so clothed the latter with gentle and amiable qualities as to enlist the feelings of all in their behalf, he would have given a false view of human nature, and his work would have lost much of its instructiveness on the score of practical morality. For good morals can never be reached by departures from truth — a rule that may be profitably remembered by all who are moved to act as advocates and special pleaders in what they think a good cause.

VII. OUTLINE OF THE STORY

Antonio, the Merchant, has a strange mood of sadness upon him, and three of his friends are bending their wits to play it off. Among them, and dearer to him than the others, is one Bassanio, a gentleman who, young and generous, has lavished his fortune. Bassanio's heart is turning towards

Portia, a wealthy heiress who, highly famed for gifts and virtues, resides not many miles off; and from whose eyes he has received "fair speechless messages." But he wants "the means to hold a rival place" among her princely suitors. Antonio freely and gladly pledges his wealth and credit to Bassanio's service, but as his funds are all embarked in ventures at sea, he tries his credit with a rich Jew, whose person he has often insulted, and whose greed his Christian liberality has often thwarted. Shylock, the Jew, feigning a merry humor, consents to lend the sum, provided Antonio sign a bond authorizing him, in case of forfeiture, to cut a pound of flesh from whatever part of his body he may choose. Antonio readily agrees to this, and so equips his friend for the loving enterprise.

Bassanio prosecutes his suit to Portia with success. But, while yet in his first transports of joy, he learns that Antonio's ventures at sea have all miscarried, and that the Jew, with malignant earnestness, claims the forfeiture. Leaving his bride the moment he has sworn the sweet oath, he hastens away, resolved to save his friend's life at the expense, if need be, of his own. Thereupon Portia gets instructions from the most learned lawyer in those parts, and, habiting herself as a doctor of laws, repairs to the trial. To divert the Jew from his purpose, she taxes her wisdom and persuasion to the utmost, but in vain. Scorning the spirit of justice, and deaf to the voice of mercy, both of which speak with eloquence from Portia's lips, rejecting thrice the amount of the bond, and standing immovable on the letter of the law, Shylock pushes his revenge to the very point of making the fatal incision, when she turns the letter of the law against him, strips him of penalty, principal, and all, and subjects even his life to the mercy of the Duke. As the condition of his life, he is required to sign a deed securing all his wealth to his daughter, who, loaded with his ducats and jewels, has lately eloped with another of Antonio's friends, and is staying at Portia's mansion during her absence. The play winds up with the hastening of all, except the Jew, to Portia's home. When all have met, Portia announces to Antonio the safe return of his ships supposed to be lost, and surprises the fugitive lovers with the news of their good fortune.

VIII. THE CHARACTERS

In respect of characterization *The Merchant of Venice* is exceedingly rich, and this too both in quantity and quality. The persons naturally fall into three several groups, with each its several plot and action ; but the three are skillfully complotted, each standing out clear and distinct in its place, yet so drawing in with the others, that everything helps on everything else, there being neither any confusion nor any appearance of care to avoid it. Of these three groups, Antonio, Shylock, and Portia are respectively the centers. The part of Lorenzo and Jessica, though strictly an episode, seems to grow forth as an element of the original germ, a sort of inherent superfluity, and as such essential to the well-being of the piece. It may be described as a fine romantic undertone accompaniment to the other parts, itself in perfect harmony with them, and perfecting their harmony with each other.

In the first entry on *The Stationers' Registers* (see above, "Date of Composition") the play is described as "a booke of the Marchaunt of Venyce or otherwise called the Jewe of Venyce." This would seem to infer that the author was then in some doubt whether to name it from Antonio or from Shylock. As an individual, Shylock is *the* character of the play, and exhibits more of mastership than any of the others; so that, viewing the persons severally, we should say the piece ought to be named from him. But we have not far to seek for good reasons why it should be named as it is. For if the Jew is the more important individually, the Merchant is so dramatically. Antonio is the center and mainspring of the action; without him, Shylock, however great in himself, had no business there. And the laws of dramatic combination, not any accident of individual prominence, are clearly what ought to govern in the naming of the play.

Antonio

Not indeed that the Merchant is a small matter in himself; far from it; he is a highly interesting and attractive personage, with timber enough in him for a good dramatic hero apart from the Jew. Something of a peculiar charm attaches to him from the state of mind in which we first see him. A dim, mysterious presage of evil weighs down his spirits, as though he felt afar off the coming on of some great calamity. This unwonted dejection, sweetened as it is with his habitual kindness and good nature, has the effect of showing how dearly he is held by such whose friendship is the fairest earthly purchase of virtue. It is significant that upon tempers like his even the smiles of fortune often have a strangely saddening effect. For such a man, even because he is good, is apt to be haunted with a sense of having more than he deserves; and this may not unnaturally inspire him with an indefinable dread of some reverse which shall square up the account of his present blessings. Thus his very happiness works by subtle methods to charge his heart with certain dark forebodings. Such presentiments are in the right line of nature:

> Oft, startled and made wise
> By their low-breathed interpretings,
> The simply-meek foretaste the springs
>   Of bitter contraries.

But the sorrow that has such noble comforters as Antonio's can hardly be ungrateful to us. Our nature is honored in the feelings that spring up on both sides.

Wealth indeed seldom dispenses such warnings save to its most virtuous possessors. And such is Antonio. A kind-hearted and sweet-mannered man; of a large and liberal spirit; affable, generous, and magnificent in his dispositions; patient of trial, indulgent to weakness, free where he loves, and frank where he hates; in prosperity modest, in adversity cheerful; craving wealth for the uses of virtue, and as the sinews of friendship; — his character is one which we never weary of contemplating. The only blemish we perceive is his treatment of Shylock: in this, though it is more the fault of the times than of the man, we cannot help siding against him. We need not ask a clearer instance of poetical justice than this, and even this we blame rather as a wrong done to himself than to Shylock; as the Jew, despite his provocations, avowedly grounds his hate mainly on those very things which make the strongest title to a good man's love. For Shylock's revenge fastens not so much on the man's abuse of him as on his kindness to others.

ANTONIO'S FRIENDS

The friendship between the Merchant and his companions is such a picture as Shakespeare evidently delighted to draw. And so fair a sentiment is not apt to inhabit ignoble breasts. Bassanio, Gratiano, and Salarino give a pleasing variety to the scenes where they move. Bassanio, though something too lavish of purse, is a model of a gentleman, in whose character and behavior all is order and propriety, with whom good manners are the proper outside and visibility of a fair mind — the natural foliage and drapery of inward refinement and delicacy and rectitude. Well-bred, he has that in him which, even had his breeding been ill, would have raised him above it and made him a gentleman.

Gratiano and Salarino are as clever, sprightly, and voluble persons as any one need desire to be with; the chief difference between them being, that the former *lets* his tongue run on from good impulses, while the latter *makes* it do so for good ends. If not so wise as Bassanio, they are more witty; and as much surpass him in strength, as they fall short of him in beauty of character. Gratiano, while much more prone than Salarino to flood us with his talk, also shows less subjection of the individual to the common forms of social decorum: so that, if he behaves not quite so well as the others, he gives livelier proof that what good behavior he has is his own — a growth from within, not a piece of imitation. And we are rather agreeably surprised that one so talkative and rattle-tongued should carry so much weight of meaning; he sometimes appears less sensible than he is, because of his galloping volubility. But he has no wish to be "reputed wise for saying nothing"; and he makes a merit of talking nonsense when, as is sometimes the case, nonsense is the best sort of sense : for, like a prime good fellow, as he is, he would rather incur the charge of folly than not, provided he can thereby add to the health and entertainment of his friends.

LORENZO AND JESSICA

Lorenzo and Jessica, the runaway lovers, are in such a lyrical state of mind that a clear view of their characters is somewhat interfered with. Both are indeed overflowing with sweetness and beauty, but more, perhaps, as the result of their relations to each other than of inherent qualities. Jessica's elopement, in itself and its circumstances, puts us to the alternative that either she is a bad child or Shylock a bad father. And while there is enough to persuade us of the latter, some share of the reproach falls to her. For if a young woman have so bad a home as to justify her in thus deserting and robbing it, the atmosphere of the place can hardly fail to leave *some* traces in her temper and character.

Lorenzo stands fair in our regard, negatively, because he does nothing unhandsome ; positively, because he has such good men for his friends. And it is rather curious that what is thus done for him, should be done for Jessica by such a person as Launcelot Gobbo. For she and the clown are made to reflect each other's choicer qualities. We think the better of her for having kindled something of poetry in such a clod, and of him for being raised above himself by such an object. Her conduct is further justified to our feelings by the odd testimony he furnishes of her father's badness; which testimony, though not of much weight in itself, goes far to confirm that of others. We see that the Jew is much the same at home as in the Rialto; that, let him be where he will, it is his nature to snarl and bite.

LAUNCELOT GOBBO

Such, from one point of view, is the dramatic propriety of this Launcelot. His part gives a fuller view both of Jessica and of her father. But, in addition to this function, he has also a value in himself. His own personal rights enter into the purpose of his introduction, and he carries in himself a part of the reason why he is so, and not otherwise; for Shakespeare seldom if ever brings in a person *merely* for the sake of others. A mixture of conceit and drollery, and hugely wrapped up in self, he is by no means a commonplace buffoon, but stands firm in his sufficiency of original stock. His elaborate nonsense, his grasping at a pun without catching it, yet feeling just as grand as if he did, is both ludicrous and natural. The poverty of his wit is enriched by his complacency in dealing it out. His part indeed amply pays its way, in showing how much of mirth may be caused by feebleness in a great attempt at a small matter. In him the mother-element of the whole piece runs out into broad humor and travesty; his reasons for breaking with his master the Jew being, as it were, a variation in drollery upon the main theme of the play. He exhibits under a comic form the general aspect of surrounding humanity; while at the same time his character is an integral part of that varied structure of human life which it belongs to the Drama to represent.

PORTIA

In Portia Shakespeare seems to have aimed at a perfect scheme of an amiable, intelligent, and accomplished woman. The result is a fine specimen of beautiful nature enhanced by beautiful art. Eminently practical in her tastes and turn of mind, full of native, home-bred sense and virtue, Portia unites therewith something of the ripeness and dignity of a sage, a mellow eloquence, and a large, noble discourse; the whole being tempered with the best grace and sensibility of womanhood. As intelligent as the strongest, she is at the same time as feminine as the weakest of her sex : she talks like a poet and a philosopher, and she talks, for all the world, just like a woman ! She is as full of pleasantry, too, and as merry "within the limit of becoming mirth," as she is womanly and wise ; and her arch sportiveness always has a special flavor as the free outcome of perfect moral health. Nothing indeed can be more fitting and well placed than her demeanor, now bracing her speech with grave maxims of practical wisdom, now unbending her mind in sallies of wit, or of innocent, roguish banter. The sportive element of her composition has its happiest showing in her dialogue with Nerissa about the "parcel of wooers," and in her humorous description of the part she imagines herself playing in her purposed disguise. The latter is especially delightful from its harmonious contrast with the solid thoughtfulness which, after all, forms the staple and frame-work of her character. How charmingly it sets off the divine rapture of eloquence with which she discourses to the Jew of mercy ! —

> I 'll hold thee any wager,
> When we are both accoutred like young men,
> I 'll prove the prettier fellow of the two,
> And wear my dagger with the braver grace;
> And speak between the change of man and boy
> With a reed voice; and turn two mincing steps
> Into a manly stride; and speak of frays,
> Like a fine-bragging youth; and tell quaint lies,
> How honourable ladies sought my love,
> Which I denying, they fell sick and died;
> I could not do withal: then I 'll repent,
> And wish, for all that, that I had not kill'd them.
> And twenty of these puny lies I 'll tell;
> Then men shall swear I have discontinued school
> Above a twelvemonth. I have within my mind
> A thousand raw tricks of these bragging Jacks,
> Which I will practise.   [III, iv, 62–78.]

Partly from condition, partly from culture, Portia has grown to live more in the understanding than in the affections; for which cause she is somewhat self-conscious, but her character is hardly the less lovely on that account; she talks considerably of herself indeed, but always so becomingly that we hardly wish her to choose any other subject, for we are pleasantly surprised that one so well aware of her gifts should still bear them so meekly. Mrs. Jameson, with Portia in her eye, intimates that Shakespeare is about the only artist, except nature, who can make women wise without turning them into men. And it is well worth the noting that, honorable as the issue of her course at the trial would be to a man, Portia shows no unwomanly craving to be in the scene of her triumph: as she goes there prompted by the feelings and duties of a wife, and for the saving of her husband's honor and peace of mind, — being resolved that "never shall he lie by Portia's side with an unquiet soul"; so she gladly leaves when these causes no longer bear in that direction. Then, too, exquisitely cultivated as she is, humanity has not been so refined out of her that in such a service she cannot stoop from her elevation, and hazard a brief departure from the sanctuary of her sex.

As Portia is to act for once the part of a man, it would seem hardly possible for her to go through the undertaking without more of self-confidence than were becoming in a woman; and the student may find plenty of matter for thought in the poet's so managing as to prevent such an impression. For there is nothing like ostentation or conceit of intellect in Portia. Though knowing enough for any station, still it never once enters her head that she is too wise for the station which Providence or the settled order of society has assigned her. She would therefore neither hide her light under a bushel that others may not see by it, nor perch it aloft in public that others may see it; but would simply set it on a candlestick that it may give light to all in her house. With her noble intellect she has gathered in the sweets of poetry and the solidities of philosophy, all for use, nothing for show; and has fairly domesticated them, has naturalized them in her sphere, and tamed them to her fireside, so that they seem as much at home there as if they had been made for no other place. And to all this mental enrichment she adds the skill

> So well to know
> Her own, that what she wills to do or say
> Seems wisest, virtuousest, discreetest, best.

Portia's consciousness of power does indeed render her cool, collected, and firm, but never a whit unfeminine: her smooth command both of herself and of the matter she goes about rather heightens our sense of her modesty than otherwise : so that the impression we take from her is, that these high mental prerogatives are of no sex ; that they properly belong to the common freehold of woman and man. Some of her speeches, especially at the trial, are evidently premeditated ; for, as any good lawyer would do, she of course prepares herself in the case beforehand ; but I should like to see the masculine lawyer that could premeditate anything equal to them.

It is to be noted withal that she goes about her work without the least misgiving as to the result ; having made herself so thoroughly familiar with both the facts and the law of the case as to feel perfectly sure on that point. Hence the charming ease and serenity with which she moves amid the excitements of the trial. No trepidations of anxiety come in to disturb the preconcerted order and method of her course. Her solemn appeals to the Jew are made in the earnest hope of inducing him to accept a full and liberal discharge of the debt. When she says to him, " there 's thrice thy money offer'd thee," it is because she really feels that both the justice of the cause and the honor of her husband would be better served by such a payment than by the more brilliant triumph which awaits her in case the Jew should spurn her offer.

Thus her management of the trial throughout is a piece of consummate art ; though of art in such a sense as presupposes perfect integrity of soul. Hence, notwithstanding her methodical forecast and preparation, she is as eloquent as an angel, and her eloquence, as by an instinctive tact, knows its time perfectly. One of her strains in this kind, her appeal to the Jew on the score of mercy, has been so often quoted, that it would long since have grown stale, if it were possible by any means to crush the freshness of unwithering youth out of it. Her style in that speech is in perfect keeping with her habitual modes of thought and discourse; even in her most spontaneous expressions we have a reflex of the same intellectual physiognomy. For the mental aptitude which she displays in the trial seems to have been the germinal idea out of which her whole part was consistently evolved; as Shakespeare's method often was, apparently, first to settle what his persons were to do, and then to conceive and work out their characters accordingly.

How nicely Shakespeare discriminates things that really differ, so as to present in all cases the soul of womanhood without a particle of effeminacy! How perfectly he reconciles things that seem most diverse, pouring into his women all the intellectual forces of the other sex, without in the least impairing or obscuring their womanliness! This is not more rare in poetry than it is characteristic of Shakespeare's workmanship. Thus Portia is as much superior to her husband in intellect, in learning, and accomplishment, as she is in wealth; but she is none the less womanly for all that. Nor does she ever on that account take the least thought of inverting the relation between them. Her mental superiority breeds no kind of social displacement, nor any desire of it. While she is acting the lawyer in disguise, her speech and bearing seem to those about her in the noblest style of manliness. In her judgelike gravity and dignity of deportment, in the extent and accuracy of her legal knowledge, in the depth and appropriateness of her moral reflections, in the luminous order and coherence and transparency of her thoughts, she suggests the worthiest of the great chief justices of history. To us who are in the secret of her sex, all the proprieties, all the inward harmonies, of her character are preserved; and the essential grace of womanhood irradiates and consecrates the dress in which she is disguised. Portia's strength and substantial dignity of character are not impaired by the romance which overflows her nature — this it is that glorifies her, and breathes enchantment about her; it adds that precious seeing to the eye which conducts her to such winning beauty and sweetness of deportment, and makes her the "rich-souled creature" that Schlegel describes her to be. In her case we have a remarkable example of how Shakespeare makes the several parts and persons of a drama cohere not only with one another but with the general circumstances wherein they occur. In Portia's character the splendor of Italian skies and scenery and art is reproduced; their spirit lives in her imagination and suffuses all she does and says.

SHYLOCK

If Portia is the beauty of this play, Shylock is its strength. In the delineation of the Jew Shakespeare had to fill with individual life and peculiarity the broad, strong outlines of national character in its most revolting form. Shylock is a true representative of his nation; wherein we have a pride which for ages never ceased to provoke hostility, but which no hostility could ever subdue, a thrift which still invited rapacity, but which no rapacity could ever exhaust, and a weakness which, while it exposed the subjects to wrong, only deepened their hate, because it kept them without the means or the hope of redress. Thus Shylock is a type of national sufferings, national sympathies, national antipathies. Himself an object of bitter insult and scorn to those about him, surrounded by enemies whom he is at once too proud to conciliate and too weak to oppose, he can have no life among them but money, no hold on them but interest, no feeling toward them but hate, no indemnity out of them but revenge. What wonder that the elements of national greatness became congealed and petrified into malignity? As avarice was the passion in which he mainly lived, the Christian virtues that thwarted this naturally seemed to him the greatest of wrongs.

With these strong national traits are interwoven personal traits equally strong. Thoroughly and intensely Jewish, he is not more a Jew than he is Shylock. In his hard, icy intellectuality, and his dry, mummylike tenacity of purpose, with a dash now and then of biting sarcastic humor, we see the remains of a great and noble nature, out of which all the genial sap of humanity has been pressed by accumulated injuries. With as much elasticity of mind as stiffness of neck, every step he takes but the last is as firm as the earth he treads upon. Nothing can daunt, nothing disconcert him; remonstrance cannot move, ridicule cannot touch, obloquy cannot exasperate him; when he has not provoked them, he has been forced to bear them; and now that he does provoke them, he is hardened against them. He may be broken; he cannot be bent.

Shylock is great in every scene where he appears, yet each later scene exhibits him in a new element or aspect of greatness. As soon as the dramatist has set forth one side or phase of his character, he forthwith dismisses that and proceeds to another. For example, the Jew's cold and penetrating sagacity, as also his malignant and remorseless guile, are effectively shown in the scene with Antonio and Bassanio, where he is first solicited for the loan. And the strength and vehemence of passion, which underlies these qualities, is still better displayed, if possible, in the scene with Antonio's two friends, Salanio and Salarino, where Shylock first avows his purpose of exacting the forfeiture. One passage of this scene has a peculiarly idiomatic strain of eloquence, steeped in a mixture of gall and pathos :

He hath disgrac'd me, and hinder'd me half a million ; laugh'd at my losses, mock'd at my gains, scorn'd my nation, thwarted my bargains, cool'd my friends, heated mine enemies ; and what 's his reason ? I am a Jew. Hath not a Jew eyes ? hath not a Jew hands, organs, dimensions, senses, affections, passions ? fed with the same food, hurt with the same weapons, subject to the same diseases, heal'd by the same means, warm'd and cool'd by the same winter and summer, as a Christian is ? If you prick us, do we not bleed ? if you tickle us, do we not laugh ? if you poison us, do we not die ? and if you wrong us, shall we not revenge ? if we are like you in the rest, we will resemble you in that. If a Jew wrong a Christian, what is his humility ? Revenge. If a Christian wrong a Jew, what should his sufferance be by Christian example ? Why, revenge. The villainy you teach me, I will execute ; and it shall go hard but I will better the instruction. [III, i, 47–63.]

National and individual traits in Shylock are so attempered and fused together that we cannot distinguish their respective influence. Even his avarice has a smack of patriotism. Money is the only defense of his brethren as well as of himself, and he craves it for their sake as well as his own ; he feels indeed that wrongs are offered to them

in him, and to him in them. Antonio has scorned his religion, balked him of usurious gains, insulted his person:
therefore he hates him as a Christian, himself a Jew; hates
him as a lender of money gratis, himself a griping usurer;
hates him as Antonio, himself Shylock. And who but a
Christian, one of Antonio's faith and fellowship, has stolen
away his daughter's heart, and drawn her into revolt, loaded
with his ducats and his precious, precious jewels?

His religion, his patriotism, his avarice, his affection, all
unite to stimulate his enmity; and his personal hate thus
reënforced overcomes for once his greed, and he grows
generous in the prosecution of his aim. The only reason he
will vouchsafe for taking the pound of flesh is, "if it will
feed nothing else, it will feed my revenge"; a reason all
the more satisfactory to him, in that those to whom he gives
it can neither allow it nor refute it; and until they can rail
the seal from off his bond, all their railings are but a fore-
taste of the revenge he seeks. In his eagerness to taste
that morsel, sweeter to him than all the luxuries of Italy, his
recent afflictions, the loss of his daughter, his ducats, his
jewels, and even the precious ring given him by his departed
wife, all fade from his mind. In his inexorable and imper-
turbable hardness at the trial there is something that makes
the blood to tingle. It is the sublimity of malice. We feel
that the yearnings of revenge have silenced all other cares
and all other thoughts. In his rapture of hate the man has
grown superhuman, and his eyes seem all aglow with preter-
natural malignity. Fearful, however, as is his passion, he
comes not off without moving our pity. In the very act
whereby he thinks to avenge his own and his brethren's
wrongs, the national curse overtakes him. In standing up

for the letter of the law against all the pleadings of mercy, he has strengthened his enemies' hands, and sharpened their weapons, against himself; and the terrible Jew sinks at last into the poor, pitiable, heartbroken Shylock.

Early in the play, when Shylock is bid forth to Bassanio's supper, and Launcelot urges him to go, because "my young master doth expect your reproach," Shylock replies, "So do I his." Of course he expects the reproach through the bankruptcy of Antonio. This would seem to infer that Shylock has some hand in getting up the reports of Antonio's "losses at sea," some of which turn out false in the end. Further than this, the poet leaves us in the dark as to how those reports grew into being and gained belief. Did he mean to have it understood that the Jew exercised his cunning and malice in plotting and preparing them? It appears that Shylock knew they were coming before they came. The natural impression from the play is that he lent the ducats and took the bond, on a mere chance of coming at his wish. But he would hardly grasp so eagerly at a bare possibility of revenge, without using means to turn it into something more. This would mark him with much deeper lines of guilt. Why, then, did not Shakespeare bring the matter forward more prominently? Perhaps it was because the doing so would have made Shylock appear too deep a criminal for the degree of interest which his part was meant to carry in the play. In other words, the health of the drama as a work of *comic* art required his criminality to be kept in the background. He comes very near overshadowing the other characters too much, as it is. And Shylock's character is *essentially tragic;* there is none of the proper timber of comedy in him.

IX. CONCLUSION

The Merchant of Venice is justly distinguished among Shakespeare's dramas, not only for the general felicity of the language, but also for the beauty of particular scenes and passages. For descriptive power, the opening scene of Antonio and his friends is not easily rivaled, and can hardly fail to live in the memory of any one having an eye for such things. Equally fine in its way is the scene of Tubal and Shylock, where the latter is so torn with the struggle of conflicting passions; his heart now sinking with grief at the account of his fugitive daughter's expenses, now leaping with malignant joy at the report of Antonio's losses. The trial scene, with its tugging vicissitudes of passion, and its hush of terrible expectation — now ringing with the Jew's sharp, spiteful snaps of malice, now made musical with Portia's strains of eloquence, now holy with Antonio's tender breathings of friendship, and dashed, from time to time, with Gratiano's fierce jets of wrath, and fiercer jets of mirth — is hardly surpassed in tragic power anywhere; and as it forms the catastrophe proper, so it concentrates the interest of the whole play. Scarcely inferior in its kind is the night scene of Lorenzo and Jessica, bathed as it is in love, moonlight, " touches of sweet harmony," and soul-lifting discourse, followed by the grave moral reflections of Portia, as she approaches her home, and sees its lights and hears its music. The bringing in of this passage of ravishing lyrical sweetness, so replete with the most soothing and tranquilizing effect, close upon the intense dramatic excitement of the trial scene, is such a transition as we shall hardly meet with but in Shakespeare, and shows his mastery of the mind's capacity of delight. The affair of the rings, with the harmless perplexities growing out of it, is a well-managed device for letting the mind down from the tragic height whereon it lately stood to the merry conclusion which the play requires. Critics indeed may easily quarrel with this sportive afterpiece ; but it stands approved by the tribunal to which criticism itself must bow — the spontaneous feelings of such as are willing to be made cheerful and healthy, without beating their brains about the *how* and *wherefore*.

What a wide diversity of materials this play reconciles and combines ! One can hardly realize how many things are here brought together, they are ordered in such perfect concert and harmony. The greatness of the work is thus hidden in its fine proportions. In many of Shakespeare's dramas we are surprised at the great variety of character : here, besides this, we have a remarkable variety of plot. And, admirable as may be the skill displayed in the characters individually considered, the interweaving of so many several plots, without the least confusion or embarrassment, evinces a still higher mastership. For, many and various as are the forms and aspects of life here shown, they all emphatically live together, as if they all had but one vital circulation.

ABBREVIATIONS USED IN THE NOTES

Q$_1$ = First Quarto, 1600.
Q$_2$ = Second Quarto, 1600.
Q$_3$ = Third Quarto, 1637.
Q$_4$ = Fourth Quarto, 1652.
Qq = all the Quartos from 1600 to 1652.
F$_1$ = First Folio, 1623.
F$_2$ = Second Folio, 1632.
F$_3$ = Third Folio, 1664.
F$_4$ = Fourth Folio, 1685.
Ff = all the seventeenth century Folios.
Rowe = Rowe's editions, 1709, 1714.
Pope = Pope's editions, 1723, 1728.
Johnson = Johnson's edition, 1765.
Camb = Cambridge edition (W. A. Wright), 1891.
Clar = Clarendon Press edition (Clark and Wright), 1869.
Furness = H. H. Furness's *A New Variorum. The Merchant of Venice*, 1888.
Abbott = E. A. Abbott's *A Shakespearian Grammar*.
Schmidt = Schmidt's *Shakespeare Lexicon*.
Skeat = Skeat's *An Etymological Dictionary*.
Murray = *A New English Dictionary* (*The Oxford Dictionary*).
Century = *The Century Dictionary*.

Other abbreviations are either self-explanatory or such as are in common use.

CHRONOLOGICAL CHART

Except in the case of Shakespeare's plays (see note) the literature dates refer to first publication

YEAR	SHAKESPEARE		BRITISH AND FOREIGN LITERATURE	HISTORY AND BIOGRAPHY
	BIOGRAPHY: POEMS	PLAYS		
1564	Birth, Baptism, April 26, Stratford-on-Avon		Quart livre de Pantagruel	Michelangelo died. Calvin died. Marlowe born. Galileo born
1565	Father became alderman		Sackville and Norton's Gorboduc printed	Philip II of Spain gave his name to Philippine Islands
1566	Brother Gilbert born		Udall's Roister Doister printed?	Murder of Rizzio
1568	Father, as bailiff of Stratford, entertained Queen's and Earl of Worcester's actors		The Bishops' Bible. La Taille's Saül. Fureux. R. Grafton's Chronicle	Mary of Scots a prisoner in England. Ascham died. Coverdale died. Netherlands War of Liberation
1572		NOTE. The plays in the columns below are arranged in the probable, though purely conjectural, order of composition. Dates appended to plays are those of first publication. Where no date is given, the play was first published in the First Folio (1623). M signifies that the play was mentioned by Meres in the **Palladis Tamia** (1598)	Camoens' Os Lusiadas (The Lusiads)	Knox died. Massacre of St. Bartholomew
1573			Tasso's Aminta	Ben Jonson born? Donne born
1574	Brother Richard born		Mirror for Magistrates (third edition)	Earl of Leicester's players licensed
1575			Gammer Gurton's Needle. Golding's Ovid (complete)	Queen Elizabeth at Kenilworth. Palissy lectured on Natural History
1576			The Paradise of Dainty Devices. Gascoigne's Steel Glass	"The Theatre" opened in Finsbury Fields, London, followed by "The Curtain." Hans Sachs died
1577	Father in financial difficulties		Holinshed's Chronicle	Drake sailed to circumnavigate globe

	Comedies	Histories	Tragedies		
1579				Gosson's School of Abuse. North's Plutarch. Lyly's Euphues (pt. i). Spenser's Shepherd's Calendar	Union of Utrecht. Tasso put in confinement at Ferrara
Sister Ann died (aged eight)					
1580				Montaigne's Essais (first edition)	Brown founded Separatists. Camoens died
Brother Edmund born					
1581				Tasso's Gerusalemme Liberata	Dutch Declaration of Independence
1582				The Rheims New Testament	Accademia della Crusca founded
Married Anne Hathaway					
1583				Garnier's Les Juives	Sir Humphrey Gilbert drowned
Daughter Susanna born					
1584				Lyly's Campaspe. Peele's Arraignment of Paris	William the Silent assassinated. Ivan the Terrible died
1585				Guarini's Pastor Fido (1590)	Ronsard died
Twin children (Hamnet, Judith) born					
1586				Camden's Britannia	Sir Philip Sidney killed
Probably went to London					
1587				Hakluyt's Four Voyages. Faustbuch (Spiess, Frankfort)	Execution of Mary of Scots
1588				Martin Marprelate: The Epistle	Defeat of Spanish Armada
1589				Puttenham's Art of English Poesie	Henry of Navarre, King of France. Palissy died in Bastille
1590	Love's Labour's Lost (M, 1598)			Marlowe's Tamburlaine. Spenser's Faerie Queene, I.-III. Lodge's Rosalynde. Sidney's Arcadia	Battle of Ivry
1591	Comedy of Errors (M)	1 Henry VI 2 Henry VI		Sidney's Astrophel and Stella. Harington's tr. of Orlando Furioso	Herrick born

CHRONOLOGICAL CHART (CONTINUED)

YEAR	SHAKESPEARE			BRITISH AND FOREIGN LITERATURE	HISTORY AND BIOGRAPHY
	BIOGRAPHY; POEMS	PLAYS (see note above)			
1592	Greene's attack in Groatsworth of Wit	Two Gentlemen of Verona (M)	Richard III (M, 1597). 3 Henry VI	**Romeo and Juliet** (M, 1597)	Daniel's Delia. Lyly's Gallathea (Galatea)	Greene died. Montaigne died. London theatres closed through plague
1593	Venus and Adonis (seven editions, 1593–1602)		King John (M). Richard II (M, 1597)	**Titus Andronicus** (M, 1594)	Peele's Edward I. Barnes's Sonnets	Marlowe died. Herbert born
1594	Lucrece (five editions, 1594–1616)	A Midsummer Night's Dream (M, 1600)			Rinuccini's Dafne. Satire Ménipée	Palestrina ("Princeps Musicæ") died
1595	Valuable contemporary references to Shakespeare	All's Well that Ends Well. Taming of the Shrew			Peele's Old Wives' Tale. Spenser's Epithalamion	Tasso died. Sir Walter Raleigh's expedition to Guiana. Sir J. Hawkins died
1596	Son Hamnet died. Family applied for coat-of-arms		1 Henry IV (M, 1598). 2 Henry IV (1600)		Drayton's Mortimeriados. Faerie Queene, Books IV–VI	Burbage built Blackfriar's Theatre. Descartes born. Sir F. Drake died
1597	Purchased New Place, Stratford	Merry Wives of Windsor, Merchant of Venice (M, 1600)			Bacon's Essays (first edition). Hall's Virgidemiarum	The Tyrone rebellion
1598	Shakespeare acted in Jonson's Every Man in His Humour	Much Ado About Nothing (1600)	Henry V (1600)		Meres's Palladis Tamia. Chapman's Homer (pt. 1). Lope de Vega's Arcadia	Peele died. Edict of Nantes
1599	Part proprietor of Globe Theatre. Coat-of-arms granted. The Passionate Pilgrim	As You Like It			Aleman's Guzman de Alfarache. Peele's David and Bethsabe	Spenser died. Globe Theatre built. Oliver Cromwell born
1600	Won a London lawsuit	Twelfth Night			England's Helicon	Calderon born. Bruno died

Year	Life of Shakespeare	Plays		Plays	Contemporary Literature	Historical Events
1601	Father died. The Phœnix and Turtle			Julius Cæsar	Jonson's Poetaster	The Essex plot. Rivalry between London adult and boy actors
1602	Purchased more Stratford real estate			Hamlet (1603)	Dekker's Satiromastix	Bodleian Library founded
1603	His company acted before the Queen	Troilus and Cressida (1609)			Jonson's Sejanus	Queen Elizabeth died. Millenary Petition
1604	Sued Rogers at Stratford	Measure for Measure		Othello	Marlowe's Faustus (1588-1589)	Hampton Court Conference
1605	Godfather to William D'Avenant			Macbeth	Don Quixote (pt. x)	Gunpowder plot. Sir Thomas Browne born
1606	King Lear given before Court			King Lear (1608)	Chapman's Monsieur D'Olive	Lyly died. Corneille born
1607	Daughter Susanna married Dr. Hall			Timon of Athens	Dekker and Webster's Westward Ho!	Settlement of Jamestown
1608	Birth of granddaughter, Elizabeth Hall. Death of mother (Mary Arden)	Pericles (1609)		Antony and Cleopatra	Captain John Smith's A True Relation. Middleton's A Mad World	Milton born. Quebec founded
1609	Sonnets, A Lover's Complaint			Coriolanus	The Douai Old Testament	Separatists (Pilgrims) in Leyden
1610	Purchased more real estate	Cymbeline			Strachey's Wracke and Redemption	Henry IV (Navarre) assassinated
1611	Subscribed for better highways	Winter's Tale The Tempest			King James Bible (A.V.). Bellarmine's Puissance du Pape	Gustavus Adolphus, King of Sweden
1613	Invested in London house property. Brother Richard died		Henry VIII		Drayton's Polyolbion	Globe Theatre burned
1616	Made his will. Daughter Judith married Thomas Quiney. Died April 23 (May 3, New Style)				Captain John Smith's New England. Folio edition of Jonson's Poems. D'Aubigné's Les Tragiques (1577)	Cervantes died. Beaumont died. Baffin explores Baffin's Bay. Harvey lectured on the circulation of the blood

THE MERCHANT OF VENICE

DRAMATIS PERSONÆ[1]

THE DUKE OF VENICE.

THE PRINCE OF MOROCCO, } suitors to Portia.
THE PRINCE OF ARRAGON,

ANTONIO,[2] a merchant of Venice.

BASSANIO, his friend, suitor likewise to Portia.

SALANIO,[3]
SALARINO, } friends to Antonio and Bassanio.
GRATIANO,

LORENZO, in love with Jessica.

SHYLOCK, a rich Jew.

TUBAL, a Jew, his friend.

SALERIO,[4]

LAUNCELOT GOBBO, the clown, servant to Shylock.

OLD GOBBO, father to Launcelot.

LEONARDO, servant to Bassanio.

BALTHASAR,
STEPHANO, } servants to Portia.

PORTIA, a rich heiress.

NERISSA, her waiting-maid.[5]

JESSICA, daughter to Shylock.

Magnificoes of Venice, Officers of the Court of Justice, Jailer,
Servants to Portia, and other Attendants.

SCENE: *Partly at Venice, and partly at Belmont, the seat of Portia,
on the Continent.*

---

[1] DRAMATIS PERSONÆ. Under the title *The Actors Names* a list of
Dramatis Personæ is given in Qs. The list given above is based upon
Rowe's.

[2] ANTONIO | Anthonio QqFf.

[3] SALANIO, SALARINO | QqFf have such spellings as Solanio, Salino,
Salaryno, Salerino, Slarino, Solarino, with varying abbreviations.

[4] SALERIO. See note, p. 86, l. 214.

[5] her waiting-maid | her wayting Gentlewoman Qs.

2

ACT I

Scene I. *Venice. A street*

Enter Antonio, Salarino, *and* Salanio

Antonio. In sooth, I know not why I am so sad :
It wearies me ; you say it wearies you ;
But how I caught it, found it, or came by it,
What stuff 't is made of, whereof it is born,
I am to learn ;   5
And such a want-wit sadness makes of me
That I have much ado to know myself.

Salarino. Your mind is tossing on the ocean ;
There, where your argosies with portly sail,
Like signiors and rich burghers on the flood,   10

Act I. In Qq no division into
Acts or Scenes; in Ff into Acts only;
in Rowe first division into Scenes.

5-6. Printed as one line in Q1Q2Ff.
8. Salarino Q1Q2 | Salanio
(Sal.) Ff and so to l. 56.

1. **sooth** : truth. See Skeat.

3. **came by it.** 'To come by' a thing is to get possession of it,
to acquire it. Cf. I, ii, 8. This expression is still used colloquially.

5. **I am to learn.** See Abbott, § 405.

9. **argosies** : large merchant vessels usually carrying rich freight.
The word is probably derived from 'Ragusa,' though some authorities
(Skeat, Clark, Wright) connect it with the classical 'Argo.' It occurs
four times, in the singular, in the first scene of Marlowe's *The Jew
of Malta.*

10. **signiors.** Shakespeare uses the word 'signior' in the sense of
'lord' or 'gentleman,' and occasionally, as in *Much Ado About Nothing*
and *Othello*, as a title of customary address.—**burghers** : citizens, free-
men of a burgh. In *As You Like It*, II, i, 23, the deer in the Forest
of Arden are described as "native burghers of this desert city."

3

Or, as it were, the pageants of the sea,
Do overpeer the petty traffickers,
That curtsy to them, do them reverence,
As they fly by them with their woven wings.

SALANIO. Believe me, sir, had I such venture forth,   15
The better part of my affections would
Be with my hopes abroad. I should be still
Plucking the grass, to know where sits the wind,
Peering in maps for ports, and piers, and roads;
And every object that might make me fear   20
Misfortune to my ventures, out of doubt
Would make me sad.

SALARINO.   My wind, cooling my broth,
Would blow me to an ague, when I thought ·
What harm a wind too great might do at sea.
I should not see the sandy hour-glass run,   25
But I should think of shallows and of flats,

---

19. **Peering** F_1 | prying Q_3Q_4.—   24. **might do at sea** $Q_2FfQ_3Q_4$
and piers F_1 | for piers Q_1. | at sea, might do Q_1.

11. **pageants.** These were originally the high stages, or scaffolds, usually on wheels, on which miracle plays and shows of various kinds were given; then the plays or shows themselves.

13. **curtsy.** "Suggested by the rocking, ducking motion in the petty traffiquers caused by the wake of the argosie as it sails past them."— Furness.

15. **venture:** what is risked — exposed to "the perils of waters, winds, and rocks."— **forth.** In Shakespeare and in Elizabethan literature 'forth' is often used in the sense of 'out,' without any verb of motion. See Abbott, § 41.

17. **still:** continually. Cf. Fr. *toujours*.

18. "Take a straw and throw it up into the air,— you may see by that which way the wind is."— Selden's *Table-talk*. Country folks often hold long grass in the air to learn the wind direction.

And see my wealthy Andrew docks in sand,
Vailing her high top lower than her ribs
To kiss her burial. Should I go to church,
And see the holy edifice of stone,   30
And not bethink me straight of dangerous rocks,
Which, touching but my gentle vessel's side,
Would scatter all her spices on the stream,
Enrobe the roaring waters with my silks ;
And, in a word, but even now worth this,   35
And now worth nothing? Shall I have the thought
To think on this ; and shall I lack the thought,

---

27. **docks** QqFf | dock'd Rowe.   36. **nothing** ? Q1 | nothing. Q2Ff.
33. **her** F1 | the Q1.

27. **Andrew**. The name of the ship given in honor either of St.
Andrew, or, as is more probable, of Andrea Doria (died 1560), the
famous admiral of Genoa.—**docks**. More vivid than Rowe's 'dock'd.'
28. The image is of a ship tilted over on one side, the other side
in the air, and the topmast down in the sand. — **Vailing** : lowering.
Marlowe uses this verb (Fr. *avaler*, Lat. *ad vallem*) twice in *The Jew
of Malta*, — transitively (V, iii, 1) :

CALYMATH. Now vail your pride, you captive Christians,
               And kneel for mercy to your conquering foe ;

intransitively (II, ii, 11) :

DEL BOSCO. Our fraught is Grecians, Turks, and Afric Moors,
                For late upon the coast of Corsica,
                Because we vailed not to the Turkish fleet,
                Their creeping galleys had us in the chase.

33, 34. These graphic figures are reproduced by Scott in *Ivanhoe*,
Chapter X, where Isaac recounts to Rebecca his perils and losses
in the Gulf of Lyons.
35. Lettsom conjectures that a line has been lost here, but the
meaning becomes clear if the actor makes a gesture indicating
bulk or largeness. Shakespeare often leaves his meaning to be
interpreted in this way.

That such a thing bechanc'd would make me sad?
But tell not me; I know, Antonio
Is sad to think upon his merchandise.   40

ANTONIO.   Believe me, no : I thank my fortune for it,
My ventures are not in one bottom trusted,
Nor to one place ; nor is my whole estate
Upon the fortune of this present year :
Therefore my merchandise makes me not sad.   45

SALARINO.   Why, then you are in love.

ANTONIO.   Fie, fie !

SALARINO.   Not in love neither. Then let us say you are sad,
Because you are not merry ; and 't were as easy
For you to laugh, and leap, and say you are merry,
Because you are not sad. Now, by two-headed Janus,   50
Nature hath fram'd strange fellows in her time :
Some that will evermore peep through their eyes,
And laugh like parrots at a bag-piper ;
And other of such vinegar aspect,

---

46. SALARINO (Salar.) Q1 | Sala-   47. neither: Q2F1Q3Q4 | neither?
nio (Sola.) Q2Ff.   Q1 | neither ! F2.

42. **bottom** : merchant ship.

46. Dyce says : "I have little doubt that Shakespeare wrote, '*In love!* fie, fie !'" This would make a normal blank verse line.

50. Janus, as the ancient Italian god who represents the spirit of opening — the opening day, the opening year (*Janu*-ary) — was the tutelary deity of gates and archways. As every gate looks two ways, Janus was often represented with a double face, one on either side of his head. Occasionally a grave face would be associated with a laughing one ; hence the peculiar propriety and significance of 'two-headed' in Salarino's oath.

54. **other.** An old plural form found often in Middle and Eliza-bethan English, the result of the final *e* dropping away from *othere* (*othre*). Cf. *Job*, xxiv, 24; *The Comedy of Errors*, IV, iii, 5.

That they'll not show their teeth in way of smile,   55
Though Nestor swear the jest be laughable.

Enter BASSANIO, LORENZO, *and* GRATIANO

SALANIO. Here comes Bassanio, your most noble kins-
    man,
Gratiano, and Lorenzo. Fare ye well :
We leave you now with better company.
SALARINO. I would have stay'd till I had made you
    merry,   60
If worthier friends had not prevented me.
ANTONIO. Your worth is very dear in my regard.
I take it, your own business calls on you,
And you embrace the occasion to depart.
SALARINO. Good morrow, my good lords.   65
BASSANIO. Good signiors both, when shall we laugh?
    say, when?
You grow exceeding strange : must it be so?
SALARINO. We'll make our leisures to attend on yours.
    [*Exeunt* SALARINO *and* SALANIO]

56. Nestor was the oldest and gravest of the Greek heroes in the
Trojan war. The severest faces might justly laugh at what he
should pronounce laughable.

61. **prevented** : anticipated. Often so in the Bible (King James
version) and Book of Common Prayer. Words derived from Latin
and Greek are almost always used by Shakespeare and Elizabethan
writers in a signification peculiarly close to the root-notion of the
word. So in this first scene of the play we have 'mortifying' (l. 82),
in the sense of 'causing death,' and 'conceit' (l. 92), in the sense of
'thought,' 'understanding.'

67. **exceeding strange.** Compare the colloquial expression, "You're
quite a stranger."

LORENZO. My Lord Bassanio, since you have found Antonio,
We two will leave you; but, at dinner-time,   70
I pray you, have in mind where we must meet.

BASSANIO. I will not fail you.

GRATIANO. You look not well, Signior Antonio;
You have too much respect upon the world:
They lose it that do buy it with much care.   75
Believe me, you are marvellously chang'd.

ANTONIO. I hold the world but as the world, Gratiano;
A stage, where every man must play a part,
And mine a sad one.

GRATIANO.   Let me play the fool:
With mirth and laughter let old wrinkles come;   80
And let my liver rather heat with wine
Than my heart cool with mortifying groans.
Why should a man, whose blood is warm within,
Sit like his grandsire cut in alabaster?
Sleep when he wakes, and creep into the jaundice   85
By being peevish? I tell thee what, Antonio, —
I love thee, and it is my love that speaks, —
There are a sort of men whose visages
Do cream and mantle like a standing pond;
And do a wilful stillness entertain,   90
With purpose to be dress'd in an opinion

78. man Q_2FfQ$_3$Q$_4$ | one Q_1.   89. cream Q_2FfQ$_3$Q$_4$ | dream Q_1.
84. alabaster | alablaster QqFf.

79. play the fool: act the part of a jester. Shakespeare draws
many impressive illustrations from the trade of the professional
'fool' — so important a character in the old comedies. Cf. *Sonnets*,
CXVI, 9; *2 Henry IV*, II, ii, 154.

82. mortifying: causing death. See note, p. 7, l. 61.

91. opinion: reputation. So also in l. 102.

Of wisdom, gravity, profound conceit;
As who should say, ' I am Sir Oracle,
And when I ope my lips, let no dog bark ! '
O my Antonio, I do know of these,   95
That therefore only are reputed wise
For saying nothing; when, I am very sure,
If they should speak, would almost damn those ears,
Which, hearing them, would call their brothers fools.
I 'll tell thee more of this another time :   100
But fish not, with this melancholy bait,
For this fool gudgeon, this opinion.

93. **am Sir** Qq | am Sir an Ff.   97. **when** QqFf | who Rowe.
95. **these** $Q_2FfQ_3Q_4$ | those Q_1.   98. **damn** F_4 | dam $Q_1Q_2F_1$.

92. **conceit**: thoughtfulness. See note, p. 7, l. 61.

93. **As who should say.** Abbott, § 257. — **Sir Oracle** : one who
thinks himself possessed of oracular or prophetic wisdom, a wise-
acre. With regard to the expression compare Sir Valour in *Troilus
and Cressida*, I, iii, 176, Sir Prudence in *The Tempest*, II, i, 286, and
Sir Smile in *The Winter's Tale*, I, ii, 196.

97. Rowe substituted ' who ' for ' when,' thus furnishing an obvious
nominative for ' would ' in the following line, but in Shakespeare
and other Elizabethan writers the nominative is often omitted when
the meaning is clear without it.

99. Referring to the judgment pronounced in the Gospel against
him who says to his brother, "Thou fool." The meaning obviously
is, that if those who "only are reputed wise for saying nothing"
should go to talking, they would be apt to damn their hearers by
provoking them to utter this reproach. A thing is often said to ' do '
that which it any way ' causes to be done.' In Shakespeare are
many instances of such usage, as in *Hamlet*, III, iv, 42. So in
the text, ' damn ' is a causative verb, and the meaning is — would almost
cause those hearers to be damned.

101, 102. Do not bait your hook with this melancholy to catch
this worthless fish. ' Gudgeon' is the name of a small fish very easily
caught, which none but fools would care to catch.

Come, good Lorenzo.   Fare ye well awhile :
I 'll end my exhortation after dinner.

LORENZO.   Well, we will leave you, then, till dinner-time.   105
I must be one of these same dumb wise men,
For Gratiano never lets me speak.

GRATIANO.   Well, keep me company but two years moe,
Thou shalt not know the sound of thine own tongue.

ANTONIO.   Farewell : I 'll grow a talker for this gear.   110

GRATIANO.   Thanks, i' faith ; for silence is only com-
      mendable
In a neat's tongue dried, and a maid not vendible.

> [*Exeunt* GRATIANO *and* LORENZO]

ANTONIO.   Is that any thing now?

BASSANIO.   Gratiano speaks an infinite deal of nothing,
more than any man in all Venice.   His reasons are as two
grains of wheat hid in two bushels of chaff : you shall seek
all day ere you find them ; and when you have them, they
are not worth the search.   118

ANTONIO.   Well, tell me now, what lady is the same
To whom you swore a secret pilgrimage,   120
That you to-day promis'd to tell me of?

BASSANIO.   'T is not unknown to you, Antonio,
How much I have disabled mine estate,

---

108. moe (mo) QqFf | more Rowe.   115. as omitted in Ff.
113. Is that Rowe's emendation   121. of? Ff | of. Qq.
| It is that QqFf.

108. moe. So read the Quartos and Folios; Rowe substituted
'more.'   Scholars find a distinction in Middle English between the
two forms, — 'mo,' or 'moe,' being used of number and with collec-
tive nouns, 'more' having reference specifically to size.

110. gear. A word of wide, general import, often used of any
business or affair in hand.

By something showing a more swelling port
Than my faint means would grant continuance :   125
Nor do I now make moan to be abridg'd
From such a noble rate ; but my chief care
Is, to come fairly off from the great debts,
Wherein my time, something too prodigal,
Hath left me gag'd. To you, Antonio,   130
I owe the most, in money and in love ;
And from your love I have a warranty
To unburthen all my plots and purposes
How to get clear of all the debts I owe.

    ANTONIO. I pray you, good Bassanio, let me know it ; 135
And if it stand, as you yourself still do,
Within the eye of honour, be assur'd,
My purse, my person, my extremest means,
Lie all unlock'd to your occasions.

    BASSANIO. In my school-days, when I had lost one shaft, 140
I shot his fellow of the selfsame flight

    126. "*To* was originally used not with the infinitive but with the
gerund in *-e*, and denoted a purpose. Gradually, as *to* superseded
the proper infinitival inflection, *to* was used in other and more indefinite senses." — Abbott.

    130. gag'd : pledged. So in *1 Henry IV*, I, iii, 172, 173 :

> That men of your nobility and power
> Did gage them both in an unjust behalf.

    137. Within the eye of honour : within the range of what may be
regarded as honorable. Cf. *The Winter's Tale*, III, ii, 52.

    141. his. The form 'its' was just creeping into use in Shakespeare's
day. It does not occur once in the Bible (King James version) as
originally printed. — Arrows were of various lengths, weights, and
featherings for different ranges, and 'flight' seems to have been a tech-
nical expression in archery with reference to range. A 'shaft of the
selfsame flight' means an arrow made for shooting the same distance.

The selfsame way with more advised watch,
To find the other forth ; and, by adventuring both,
I oft found both. I urge this childhood proof,
Because what follows is pure innocence.   145
I owe you much ; and, like a wilful youth,
That which I owe is lost : but, if you please
To shoot another arrow that self way
Which you did shoot the first, I do not doubt,
As I will watch the aim, or to find both,   150
Or bring your latter hazard back again,
And thankfully rest debtor for the first.

    ANTONIO. You know me well; and herein spend but
        time
To wind about my love with circumstance ;
And out of doubt you do me now more wrong   155
In making question of my uttermost,
Than if you had made waste of all I have :
Then do but say to me what I should do,
That in your knowledge may by me be done,
And I am prest unto it : therefore, speak.   160

    BASSANIO. In Belmont is a lady richly left ;
And she is fair, and, fairer than that word,

---

155. do me now Qq | do to me F2F3F4 | do F1.

143. forth : out. See note, p. 4, l. 15.
144. childhood proof : childish instance or experiment. Similarly,
"childhood innocence" in *A Midsummer Night's Dream*, III, ii, 202.
146. wilful. Warburton suggested 'witless,' and Collier 'wasteful,'
as substitutes for ' wilful,' but the text needs no emendation.
154. circumstance : circumlocution. Cf. *The Comedy of Errors*, V,
i, 19; *Two Gentlemen of Verona*, I, i, 40 ; *Hamlet*, I, v, 127.
160. prest : ready (Fr. *prêt*, Lat. *praesto*).
162. She is beautiful and has what is better than beauty.

Of wondrous virtues : sometimes from her eyes
I did receive fair speechless messages.
Her name is Portia; nothing undervalu'd   165
To Cato's daughter, Brutus' Portia :
Nor is the wide world ignorant of her worth ;
For the four winds blow in from every coast
Renowned suitors; and her sunny locks
Hang on her temples like a golden fleece ;   170
Which makes her seat of Belmont Colchos' strand,
And many Jasons come in quest of her.
O my Antonio, had I but the means
To hold a rival place with one of them,
I have a mind presages me such thrift,   175
That I should questionless be fortunate.

 ANTONIO.   Thou know'st that all my fortunes are at sea ;
Neither have I money, nor commodity,
To raise a present sum : therefore go forth ;
Try what my credit can in Venice do :   180
That shall be rack'd, even to the uttermost,
To furnish thee to Belmont, to fair Portia.
Go, presently inquire, and so will I,
Where money is; and I no question make,
To have it of my trust, or for my sake.   [*Exeunt*] 185

171. strand Johnson | strond QqFf.   172. come Q2FfQ3Q4 | comes Q1.

163. 'Sometimes' and 'sometime' were used indifferently, and
often, as here, in the sense of 'formerly,' or 'former.'
165. nothing undervalu'd : not at all inferior in value. So, later
in this play (II, vii, 53), we have "ten times undervalu'd to tried
gold." And 'nothing' as a strong negative is very common.
178. commodity : merchandise, anything that might be pledged as
security for a loan, collateral.

Scene II. *Belmont. A room in* Portia's *house*

Enter Portia *and* Nerissa

PORTIA. By my troth, Nerissa, my little body is aweary
of this great world.

NERISSA. You would be, sweet madam, if your miseries
were in the same abundance as your good fortunes are :
and yet, for aught I see, they are as sick that surfeit with
too much, as they that starve with nothing. It is no mean
happiness, therefore, to be seated in the mean : superfluity
comes sooner by white hairs, but competency lives longer.

PORTIA. Good sentences, and well pronounc'd.   9

NERISSA. They would be better, if well follow'd.

PORTIA. If to do were as easy as to know what were
good to do, chapels had been churches, and poor men's
cottages princes' palaces. It is a good divine that follows
his own instructions : I can easier teach twenty what were
good to be done, than be one of the twenty to follow mine
own teaching. The brain may devise laws for the blood ;
but a hot temper leaps o'er a cold decree : such a hare is

5. aught | ought QqFf.   15. than be F₄ | then be F₁F₂F₃ |
6. mean Qq | small Ff.   then to be Qq.

6-8. The Folios, with their reading, "small happiness," lose the
Shakespearian play on words. Here, with 'mean' as with 'will' in
ll. 21, 22, the words are used in the double sense so dear to the
euphuistic Elizabethan. — superfluity comes, etc. One who is rich
and fares sumptuously sooner gets white hairs, grows old, and dies.
— comes by. See note on I, i, 3.

16-17. blood . . . hot temper. These were cause and effect according to the old physiologists ; hence the mediæval allegorical poets
often identify the two, and put them for passion and impulse generally — a tradition followed by the Elizabethan writers.

madness the youth, to skip o'er the meshes of good counsel
the cripple. But this reasoning is not in the fashion to
choose me a husband. O me, the word ' choose ' ! I may
neither choose whom I would, nor refuse whom I dislike ;
so is the will of a living daughter curb'd by the will of a
dead father. Is it not hard, Nerissa, that I cannot choose
one, nor refuse none?   24

NERISSA. Your father was ever virtuous ; and holy men,
at their death, have good inspirations : therefore the lottery
that he hath devis'd in these three chests of gold, silver,
and lead, — whereof who chooses his meaning chooses you,
— will, no doubt, never be chosen by any rightly, but one
who shall rightly love. But what warmth is there in your
affection towards any of these princely suitors that are
already come?   32

PORTIA. I pray thee, over-name them ; and, as thou
namest them, I will describe them ; and, according to my
description, level at my affection.

NERISSA. First, there is the Neapolitan prince.   36

PORTIA. Ay, that 's a colt indeed, for he doth nothing but

---

19. reasoning is not in the Qq |
reason is not in Ff.
23. Is it QqF$_2$F$_3$F$_4$ | it is F$_1$.

29. will, no doubt, never Q$_2$FfQ$_3$
Q$_4$ | no doubt you will never Q$_1$.
30. who Q$_1$ | who you Q$_2$FfQ$_3$Q$_4$.

19. reasoning: talk, conversation. Shakespeare uses 'reason,'
noun and verb, in this sense, II, viii, 27 ; *King Lear*, V, i, 26.

22. will. The second 'will' is 'will and testament.' In *Sonnets*,
CXXXV, CXXXVI, Shakespeare puns throughout upon the word ' Will.'

23-24. Double negatives are common in Early and Middle English.

35. level at : aim at, guess at. Cf. *2 Henry IV*, III, ii, 86. The
figure is that of leveling a weapon with a view to hit an object.

37. colt. An equivoque. 'Colt' was used for a wild, dashing,
skittish youngster. Steevens notes that in the sixteenth century the
Neapolitans were much noted for horsemanship.

talk of his horse ; and he makes it a great appropriation
to his own good parts, that he can shoe him himself.

NERISSA. Then is there the County Palatine.   40

PORTIA. He doth nothing but frown ; as who should say,
' If you will not have me, choose.' He hears merry tales,
and smiles not : I fear he will prove the weeping philosopher
when he grows old, being so full of unmannerly sadness in
his youth. I had rather be married to a death's-head with
a bone in his mouth than to either of these. God defend
me from these two !   47

NERISSA. How say you by the French lord, Monsieur
Le Bon?   49

PORTIA. God made him, and therefore let him pass for a
man. In truth, I know it is a sin to be a mocker : but, he !
why, he hath a horse better than the Neapolitan's ; a better
bad habit of frowning than the Count Palatine : he is every

---

40. **Palatine** Q1 | Palentine Q2FfQ3.   45. **be** Qq | to be Ff.

38. **appropriation.** Used oddly here in the sense of 'addition.' The
word does not occur again in Shakespeare. Collier suggested as an
emendation the substitution of 'approbation of,' Shakespeare using
'approbation' more than once in the sense of 'proof.' Q1 reads
'appropriation unto.'

43. **the weeping philosopher.** This was Heraclitus of Ephesus,
who is said to have become a complete recluse, and retreated to
the mountains, where he lived on pot-herbs. He was called "the
weeping philosopher" because he mourned over the follies of mankind, just as Democritus was called "the laughing philosopher"
because he laughed at them. Perhaps Portia has in mind the pre-
cept : "Rejoice with them that do rejoice, and weep with them that
weep." — *Romans*, xii, 15.

45. The reference is to the skull and crossbones so often sculp-
tured on tombstones.

48. **by :** about. Cf. II, ix, 25 ; *Love's Labour's Lost*, IV, iii, 150 ;
All's Well that Ends Well, V, iii, 237.

man in no man : if a throstle sing, he falls straight a-caper-
ing ; he will fence with his own shadow. If I should marry
him, I should marry twenty husbands. If he would despise
me, I would forgive him ; for, if he love me to madness, I
shall never requite him.   58

NERISSA. What say you then to Falconbridge, the young
baron of England?   60

PORTIA. You know I say nothing to him ; for he under-
stands not me, nor I him : he hath neither Latin, French,
nor Italian ; and you will come into the court and swear that
I have a poor pennyworth in the English. He is a proper
man's picture ; but, alas, who can converse with a dumb-show?

---

54. throstle | Trassell   QqF1 | 58. shall Qq | should Ff.
Tarssell F2 | Tassell, F3 | Tassel F4.

54. **throstle.** The F2 emendation, 'Tarssell' (*tiercel, tarcel,* or
tercel, a male hawk), was an unlucky attempt to hit the right bird.
'Trassell' may be no misprint, but a phonetic representation of a
pronunciation of 'throstle' still common in Scotland and the north of
England ; though in *A Midsummer Night's Dream,* III, i, 130 —

> The ousel cock so black of hue,
> With orange-tawny bill,
> The throstle with his note so true,

the word is consistently spelled 'throstle,' both in Quartos and Folios.

55–56. **I should . . . I should.** See Abbott, §§ 322–331.

59. **to:** as to, concerning. Portia in her answer uses Nerissa's
expression 'say to' punningly in its ordinary signification.

64. **proper:** well-formed. The word is still used in this sense in
certain districts in Scotland. *Hebrews,* xi, 23 : "By faith Moses,
when he was born, was hid three months of his parents, because
they saw he was a proper child." Cf. *A Midsummer Night's Dream,*
I, ii, 88 ; *2 Henry IV,* II, ii, 72 ; *As You Like It,* III, v, 51.

65. **dumb-show:** a dramatic representation, or part of one, shown
pantomimically. Dumb-shows were common in the early English
drama and were familiar to Shakespeare's audiences. A dumb-show
is introduced in *Hamlet,* III, ii, 145.

How oddly he is suited! I think he bought his doublet in
Italy, his round hose in France, his bonnet in Germany, and
his behaviour every where.   68

NERISSA. What think you of the Scottish lord, his neighbour?   70

PORTIA. That he hath a neighbourly charity in him; for
he borrow'd a box of the ear of the Englishman, and swore
he would pay him again when he was able: I think the Frenchman became his surety, and seal'd under for another.   74

69. Scottish Qq | other Ff.   72. swore F1 | sworne F2.

66. doublet : the outer body garment worn by men in the sixteenth
century, the name having reference to the heavy lining or quilting.

67. hose: very tight trousers covering the waist and legs. Foot
covering was not known by this name until after 1600.— bonnet:
common name for man's headdress in many districts of Scotland
to-day. This fashion of affecting foreign dress is satirized in a similar vein by Don Pedro in *Much Ado About Nothing*, III, ii, 33 : "A
Dutchman to-day, a Frenchman to-morrow, or in the shape of two
countries at once, as, a German from the waist downward, all slops,
and a Spaniard from the hip upward, no doublet." Such passages
resemble descriptions of Elizabethan fops and gallants in Joseph
Hall's *Satires* (*Virgidemiarum*), published in 1597–1598:

> How stiffly struts he by,
> All trapped in the new-found bravery.
> The nuns of new-won Calais his bonnet lent,
> In lieu of their so kind a conquerment.
> What needed he fetch that from farthest Spain,
> His grandame could have lent with lesser pain?

69. The Folio substitution of 'other' for the 'Scottish' of the
1600 Quartos was obviously in deference to King James I.

74. To 'seal' was to 'subscribe'; as Antonio afterwards says,
I, iii, 144, "I'll seal to such a bond." The principal sealed to a
bond, his surety sealed under. The meaning therefore is that the
Frenchman became surety for another box of the ear, to be given in
repayment of the first. There is satirical allusion here to the frequent Scottish-French alliances against England.

NERISSA. How like you the young German, the Duke of
Saxony's nephew?   76

PORTIA. Very vilely in the morning, when he is sober;
and most vilely in the afternoon, when he is drunk; when
he is best, he is a little worse than a man; and when
he is worst, he is little better than a beast: and the worst
fall that ever fell, I hope I shall make shift to go without him.   82

NERISSA. If he should offer to choose, and choose the
right casket, you should refuse to perform your father's will,
if you should refuse to accept him.   85

PORTIA. Therefore, for fear of the worst, I pray thee, set
a deep glass of Rhenish wine on the contrary casket; for,
if the devil be within and that temptation without, I know
he will choose it. I will do any thing, Nerissa, ere I 'll be
married to a sponge.   90

NERISSA. You need not fear, lady, the having any of
these lords : they have acquainted me with their determina-
tions; which is, indeed, to return to their home, and to
trouble you with no more suit, unless you may be won by
some other sort than your father's imposition depending
on the caskets.   96

---

77. vilely | vildely Q1Ff.   89. I 'll | Ile Q1 | I will Ff.

80. and. Such is the reading of Quartos and Folios. No need to
change the word to ' an.' ' And ' meaning ' if ' is common in Middle
and Elizabethan English, as well as in colloquial and provincial use
to-day. See Abbott, §§ 101, 103.

91. the having. See Abbott, § 93.

95. sort. Here used in the sense of ' lot '; from the Latin *sors*. So
in *Troilus and Cressida*, I, iii, 376: "let blockish Ajax draw The
sort to fight with Hector." — your father's imposition : the conditions imposed by your father.

PORTIA. If I live to be as old as Sibylla, I will die as chaste as Diana, unless I be obtain'd by the manner of my father's will. I am glad this parcel of wooers are so reasonable; for there is not one among them but I dote on his very absence; and I pray God grant them a fair departure.   102

NERISSA. Do you not remember, lady, in your father's time, a Venetian, a scholar, and a soldier, that came hither in company of the Marquis of Montferrat?   105

---

101. **pray God grant** Qq | wish   104. **Venetian, a scholar** Q2FfQ3
F1F2.   Q4 | Venetian scholler Q1.

---

97. Shakespeare here turns the word 'sibyl' into a proper name. That he knew it to be a generic, not an individual name, appears in *Othello*, III, iv, 70:

> A sibyl, that had number'd in the world,
> The sun to course two hundred compasses,
> In her prophetic fury sew'd the work.

Bacon, in his essay, *Of Delays*, also uses the word as a proper name : "Fortune is like the market where, many times, if you can stay a little, the price will fall. And again, it is sometimes like *Sybilla's* offer, which at first offereth the commodity at full, then consumeth part and part, and still holdeth up the price." The particular sibyl referred to by Portia is the Cumæan Sibyl, so named from Cumæ in Italy, where she had her prophetic seat. Apollo offered to grant any request she might make. Her request was that she might live as many years as the number of the grains of sand which she was grasping.

101. **I pray God grant.** So the Quartos; the Folios read, 'I wish.' The famous statute of 1605, "to restrain the abuses of Players," is perhaps responsible for this change. This statute expressly states, "that if . . . any person . . . do or shall in any Stage-play . . . use the holy Name of God . . . shall forfeit . . . ten pounds." But elsewhere in the Folio of 1623 the name of God is retained in similar expressions, I, ii, 46, 50; II, ii, 60; II, ii, 102, etc., so too much need not be made of the influence of the 1605 legislation upon this textual variation.

PORTIA. Yes, yes, it was Bassanio; as I think he was so
call'd.   107

NERISSA. True, madam : he, of all the men that ever
my foolish eyes look'd upon, was the best deserving a
fair lady.   110

PORTIA. I remember him well; and I remember him
worthy of thy praise.

Enter a Serving-man

How now ! what news?   113

SERVING-MAN. The four strangers seek for you, madam,
to take their leave : and there is a forerunner come from
a fifth, the Prince of Morocco ; who brings word, the prince
his master will be here to-night.   117

PORTIA. If I could bid the fifth welcome with so good
heart as I can bid the other four farewell, I should be glad
of his approach : if he have the condition of a saint and the
complexion of a devil, I had rather he should shrive me
than wive me.   122
Come, Nerissa. Sirrah, go before.
Whiles we shut the gates upon one wooer, another knocks
           at the door.   *[Exeunt]*

---

106. **he was so** Q1 | so was he Q2Ff
Q3Q4.
113. **How now ! what news?** Qq |
omitted in Ff.

114. **seek for you** Qq | seek you Ff.
123-124. Printed as prose in Qq
Ff | first as verse by Knight.
124. **gates** Q1 | gate Q2Q3Q4Ff.

---

114. **The four strangers.** Six have been enumerated. Most probably this is an oversight on Shakespeare's part. Attempts have been
made to saddle the mistake on careless editors and printers ; also
to found upon it a theory of a first draft of the play (or an older play)
in which were only four strangers, the English and the Scottish lords
being probably added in the revision, to please an English audience.

SCENE III. *Venice. A public place*

Enter BASSANIO *and* SHYLOCK

SHYLOCK. Three thousand ducats, — well.

BASSANIO. Ay, sir, for three months.

SHYLOCK. For three months, — well.

BASSANIO. For the which, as I told you, Antonio shall be
bound.   5

SHYLOCK. Antonio shall become bound, — well.

BASSANIO. May you stead me? will you pleasure me?
shall I know your answer?

SHYLOCK. Three thousand ducats for three months, and
Antonio bound.   10

BASSANIO. Your answer to that.

SHYLOCK. Antonio is a good man.

BASSANIO. Have you heard any imputation to the contrary?

SHYLOCK. Ho! no, no, no, no: my meaning, in saying
he is a good man, is to have you understand me, that he
is sufficient. Yet his means are in supposition: he hath
an argosy bound to Tripolis, another to the Indies; I
understand, moreover, upon the Rialto, he hath a third at
Mexico, a fourth for England; and other ventures he hath,

Enter BASSANIO ... | Enter Bas-   19-20. hath, squander'd | Theo-
sanio with Shylock the Jew QqFf.   bald inserted comma | hath squan-
                                       dered QqFf.

1. **well**. The word has here something of an interrogative force.

4. **the which**. See Abbott, § 270.

7. **May you**. 'May' originally involved the notion of ability
(Anglo-Saxon *magan*, German *mögen*). See Abbott, § 307.

18. **the Rialto**. "As it were Rivo Alto, a high shore. . . . An emi-
nent place in Venice where Merchants commonly meet." — Florio,
Italian Dictionary, 1611. See note on l. 99.

squander'd abroad. But ships are but boards, sailors but
men : there be land-rats and water-rats, water-thieves and
land-thieves, I mean pirates : and then there is the peril
of waters, winds, and rocks. The man is, notwithstanding,
sufficient. Three thousand ducats; — I think I may take
his bond.   25

BASSANIO. Be assur'd you may.

SHYLOCK. I will be assur'd I may; and, that I may be
assur'd, I will bethink me. May I speak with Antonio?

BASSANIO. If it please you to dine with us.   29

SHYLOCK. Yes, to smell pork; to eat of the habitation
which your prophet the Nazarite conjur'd the devil into. I
will buy with you, sell with you, talk with you, walk with
you, and so following; but I will not eat with you, drink
with you, nor pray with you. What news on the Rialto? —
Who is he comes here?   35

Enter ANTONIO

BASSANIO. This is Signior Antonio.

SHYLOCK. [*Aside*] How like a fawning publican he looks !
I hate him for he is a Christian ;
But more for that, in low simplicity,
He lends out money gratis and brings down   40

31. See *Matthew*, viii, 32. In all Bible translations into English
in the sixteenth century, from Tyndale's to that of the Bishops'
Bible, 'Nazarite' is used, as 'Nazarene' is in the King James version, to describe a man of Nazareth.

37. fawning publican. The explanation of this peculiar and difficult
expression may be found in *Luke*, xviii, 10–14. Professor Moulton,
Shakespeare as a Dramatic Artist, p. 61, note, suggests that this line
should be given to Antonio.

The rate of usance here with us in Venice.
If I can catch him once upon the hip,
I will feed fat the ancient grudge I bear him.
He hates our sacred nation ; and he rails,
Even there where merchants most do congregate,   45
On me, my bargains, and my well-won thrift,
Which he calls interest. Cursed be my tribe,
If I forgive him !

    BASSANIO.   Shylock, do you hear?

    SHYLOCK.   I am debating of my present store ;
And, by the near guess of my memory,   50
I cannot instantly raise up the gross
Of full three thousand ducats. What of that?
Tubal, a wealthy Hebrew of my tribe,

---

46. **well-won** Qq | well-worn Ff.   48. **Shylock** | Shyloch Q2.

41. 'Usance,' 'usury,' and 'interest' were all terms of precisely the same import in Shakespeare's time; there being then no such law or custom whereby 'usury' has since come to mean the taking of interest above a certain rate. How the taking of interest, at whatever rate, was commonly esteemed at that time is shown in Lord Bacon's essay, *Of Usurie*, where he mentions the popular arguments against it : " that the usurer is the greatest Sabbath Breaker, because his Plough goeth every Sunday . . . that the usurer breaketh the First Law, that was made for Mankind after the Fall; which was, *In sudore Vultûs tui comedes Panem tuum*.[1] . . . That usurers should have Orange-tawney Bonnets, because they do Judaize. That it is against Nature, for Money to beget Money . . ." From this it is plain that usury was regarded as a badge of Judaism.

42. **upon the hip.** Some explain this as a phrase of wrestling; others, of hunting. To 'have one on the hip' was to have the advantage. Henley thinks the explanation of the expression may be found in *Genesis*, xxxii, 24–32. Cf. IV, i, 329, and *Othello*, II, i, 314.

[1] In the sweat of thy face shalt thou eat thy bread.

Will furnish me. But, soft ! how many months
Do you desire? — [*To* ANT.] Rest you fair, good signior ;
Your worship was the last man in our mouths.   56

   ANTONIO. Shylock, although I neither lend nor borrow,
By taking nor by giving of excess,
Yet, to supply the ripe wants of my friend,
I 'll break a custom. — Is he yet possess'd   60
How much ye would?

   SHYLOCK.   Ay, ay, three thousand ducats.

   ANTONIO. And for three months.

   SHYLOCK. I had forgot, — three months ; you told me so.
Well then, your bond ; and, let me see ; but hear you ;
Methought you said you neither lend nor borrow   65
Upon advantage.

   ANTONIO.   I do never use it.

   SHYLOCK. When Jacob graz'd his uncle Laban's sheep, —
This Jacob from our holy Abram was

---

55. [*To* ANT.] Rowe.

57. **although** Q1 | albeit Q2FfQ3
Q4.

59. **ripe** QqFf | rife Johnson conj.

60-61. Is he . . . ye would Q2Q3Q4
| are you resolv'd, How much he
would have Q1 | is he yet possest
How much he would Ff.

55. **Rest you fair** : good health to you ! may you continue well !
— a conventional greeting where 'God' may be understood as the subject of 'rest,' as in the common Elizabethan wish, especially at part-
ing, "God rest you merry !" Cf. *As You Like It*, V, i, 65.

60-61. **Is he yet possess'd How much ye would ?** This is the reading
of the Second Quarto, and Furnivall calls it the test passage in deter-
mining the superiority of this Quarto to the First. Furness prefers and
defends the reading of the First Quarto, adding at the close of his
argument, " if, however, the text of Q2 is to be preferred, I should
certainly change the *ye*, not into *you*, as Theobald changed it, but
into *we*, as suggested by Walker and adopted by Dyce and Hudson." [1]
The Folio reading is obviously a mistake. — **possess'd** : informed.

---

[1] In the earlier editions of Hudson's Shakespeare.

(As his wise mother wrought in his behalf)
The third possessor ; ay, he was the third, —   70
    ANTONIO. And what of him? did he take interest?

    SHYLOCK. No, not take interest ; not, as you would say,
Directly interest : mark what Jacob did.
When Laban and himself were compromis'd
That all the eanlings which were streak'd and pied   75
Should fall as Jacob's hire,
The skilful shepherd pill'd me certain wands ;
He stuck them up before the fulsome ewes,
Who, then conceiving, did in eaning time
Fall parti-colour'd lambs, and those were Jacob's.   80
This was a way to thrive, and he was blest :
And thrift is blessing, if men steal it not.

    ANTONIO. This was a venture, sir, that Jacob serv'd for ;
A thing not in his power to bring to pass,
But sway'd and fashion'd by the hand of heaven.   85
Was this inserted to make interest good?
Or is your gold and silver ewes and rams?

    SHYLOCK. I cannot tell ; I make it breed as fast.
But note me, signior.

70. third, — Dyce | third. QqFf.   77. pill'd | pil'd F_1 | peel'd Pope.

70. **The third possessor.** Reckoning Abraham himself as the first.
How Jacob's " wise mother wrought " is told in *Genesis*, xxvii.

75. **eanlings :** newborn lambs. — **pied :** spotted.

77. **me.** This is the ethical dative, with the force of 'mark me
well,' as in *1 Henry IV*, II, iv, 233, 241. See Abbott, § 220.

79. **eaning time :** lambing season. From Anglo-Saxon *eánian*,
'bring forth.'

86. Was this inserted in Scripture?

86, 88. " The Greek word for interest, τόκος, is the exact equivalent
of the English word *breed*, and the idea underlying the two was
regularly connected with that of interest in ancient discussions. The

ANTONIO.   Mark you this, Bassanio,
The devil can cite Scripture for his purpose.   90
An evil soul, producing holy witness,
Is like a villain with a smiling cheek;
A goodly apple rotten at the heart:
O, what a goodly outside falsehood hath!   94
    SHYLOCK. Three thousand ducats,—'t is a good round sum.
Three months from twelve, — then, let me see; the rate —
    ANTONIO. Well, Shylock, shall we be beholding to you?
    SHYLOCK. Signior Antonio, many a time and oft
In the Rialto you have rated me   99

---

94. goodly QqFf | godly Rowe | comely Bailey conj.

96. then, let me see; the rate — Camb | then let me see the rate. QqFf.

same idea is present throughout the dispute between Antonio and Shylock. . . . They considered the distinction between the using of flesh and metal for the medium of wealth to be the essential point in their dispute." — Moulton, *Shakespeare as a Dramatic Artist*, p. 63. Hence, according to Moulton, the root-idea of the conversation flashes into Shylock's mind the idea of the bond.

90. Cf. *The Jew of Malta*, I, ii, 112:

What, bring you Scripture to confirm your wrongs?

94. goodly. Rowe substituted 'godly.' Walker made the same change, remarking that 'goodly' and 'godly,' and, in like manner, 'good' and 'God,' have been confounded in various passages of old English writers. Dyce held that the 'goodly' of Quartos and Folios was repeated from the preceding line by a printer's mistake.

97. beholding: beholden. A common sixteenth century corruption.

99. Rialto. In this scene we have already had "on the Rialto" and "upon the Rialto." Concerning the place meant, Rogers thus speaks in one of the notes to his poem on Italy: "Rialto is the name, not of the bridge, but of the island from which it is called; and the Venetians say *il ponte di Rialto*, as we say Westminster-bridge. In that island is the exchange; and I have often walked there as on classic ground. In the days of Antonio and Bassanio it was second to none." See note on l. 18.

About my moneys and my usances :   100
Still have I borne it with a patient shrug ;
For sufferance is the badge of all our tribe.
You call me misbeliever, cut-throat dog,
And spit upon my Jewish gaberdine,
And all for use of that which is mine own.   105
Well then, it now appears you need my help :
Go to, then ; you come to me, and you say,
' Shylock, we would have moneys : ' you say so ;
You, that did void your rheum upon my beard,
And foot me as you spurn a stranger cur   110
Over your threshold : moneys is your suit.
What should I say to you? Should I not say,
' Hath a dog money? is it possible
A cur can lend three thousand ducats? ' or
Shall I bend low, and in a bondman's key,   115
With bated breath and whispering humbleness,
Say this, —
' Fair sir, you spit on me on Wednesday last ;
You spurn'd me such a day ; another time
You call'd me dog ; and for these courtesies   120
I 'll lend you thus much moneys '?

    ANTONIO. I am as like to call thee so again,
To spit on thee again, to spurn thee too.
If thou wilt lend this money, lend it not

104. spit F₃F₄ | spet QqF₁F₂.   118. spit | spet QqFf.
114. can Qq | should Ff.   119. day ; another time Ff | day
117-118. Printed as one line in   another time Qq.
QqFf.   123. too Ff | to Qq.

    104. **gaberdine** : a long, coarse outer garment or frock. Caliban,
in *The Tempest*, II, ii, 40, wears one big enough, it seems, to wrap
both himself and Trinculo in.

As to thy friends ; for when did friendship take   125
A breed of barren metal of his friend?
But lend it rather to thine enemy ;
Who if he break, thou mayst with better face
Exact the penalty.

SHYLOCK.   Why, look you, how you storm !
I would be friends with you, and have your love,   130
Forget the shames that you have stain'd me with,
Supply your present wants, and take no doit
Of usance for my moneys, and you 'll not hear me :
This is kind I offer.

BASSANIO. This were kindness.

SHYLOCK.   This kindness will I show :
Go with me to a notary, seal me there   136
Your single bond ; and, in a merry sport,
If you repay me not on such a day,
In such a place, such sum or sums as are
Express'd in the condition, let the forfeit   140
Be nominated for an equal pound
Of your fair flesh, to be cut off and taken
In what part of your body pleaseth me.

125. friends QqF₁ | friend F₂F₃F₄.   129. penalty Qq | penalties Ff.
126. breed of Ff | breed for Qq.   143. pleaseth Qq | it pleaseth Ff.

126. breed : interest ('bred' from the principal).

128. Who if he break. Doubling of the subject, 'who' and 'he,' in
relative clauses was common with Elizabethan writers. Bacon has it
often. So in *The Advancement of Learning :* "Which though it
be not true, yet I forbear to note any deficiencies." But 'who' in
this line may be equal to 'from whom.' See Abbott, § 249.

132. doit : small Dutch coin of little value.

141–142. The language is odd, and rather obscure. The sense
probably is : Let the forfeiture of a pound of your flesh be named
or specified as an equivalent for the debt.

ANTONIO. Content, in faith; I 'll seal to such a bond,
And say there is much kindness in the Jew.   145

BASSANIO. You shall not seal to such a bond for me:
I 'll rather dwell in my necessity.

ANTONIO. Why, fear not, man; I will not forfeit it:
Within these two months, that 's a month before
This bond expires, I do expect return   150
Of thrice three times the value of this bond.

SHYLOCK. O father Abram, what these Christians are,
Whose own hard dealings teaches them suspect
The thoughts of others! — Pray you, tell me this:
If he should break his day, what should I gain   155
By the exaction of the forfeiture?
A pound of man's flesh taken from a man
Is not so estimable, profitable neither,
As flesh of muttons, beefs, or goats. I say,
To buy his favour, I extend this friendship: 160
If he will take it, so; if not, adieu;
And, for my love, I pray you wrong me not.

ANTONIO. Yes, Shylock, I will seal unto this bond.

SHYLOCK. Then meet me forthwith at the notary's:
Give him direction for this merry bond;   165
And I will go and purse the ducats straight;
See to my house, left in the fearful guard

---

153. dealings teaches QqF1 | deal-
ing teaches F2F3F4.

161. it, so Q2FfQ3Q4 | it so Q1.
167. fearful | fearless Warburton.

153. **teaches.** This is probably the old Northern plural in -*s*, still
common in Scottish dialect: "when the kye comes hame." See
Abbott, § 333.

155. **break his day**: fail to pay on the day appointed.

167. **fearful guard**: a guard not to be trusted, or that gives cause
of fear. 'To fear' was used in an active as well as a passive sense.
So in the next scene: "this aspect of mine Hath fear'd the valiant."

Of an unthrifty knave ; and presently
I will be with you.

    ANTONIO.   Hie thee, gentle Jew. [*Exit* SHYLOCK]
The Hebrew will turn Christian : he grows kind.   170

    BASSANIO. I like not fair terms and a villain's mind.

    ANTONIO. Come on : in this there can be no dismay ;
My ships come home a month before the day.   [*Exeunt*]

169-170. Antonio's speech printed
as prose in QqFf.
    170. The Qq Pope Capell Camb |

This Ff.—grows kind Ff | grows so
kind Q1.
    171. terms | teames Ff.

ACT II

Scene I. *Belmont. A room in* Portia's *house*

Flourish of cornets. Enter the Prince of Morocco *and his train;* Portia, Nerissa, *and others attending*

Morocco. Mislike me not for my complexion,
The shadow'd livery of the burnish'd sun,
To whom I am a neighbour and near bred.
Bring me the fairest creature northward born,
Where Phœbus' fire scarce thaws the icicles,   5
And let us make incision for your love,
To prove whose blood is reddest, his or mine.
I tell thee, lady, this aspect of mine
Hath fear'd the valiant: by my love, I swear
The best-regarded virgins of our clime   10
Have lov'd it too. I would not change this hue,
Except to steal your thoughts, my gentle queen.

4. **Bring me the** Ff | bring the Q1.   11. **Have** Ff | Hath Q1.

1. The old stage direction introducing this second scene and its characters contains a graphic description of the Prince of Morocco: "Enter Morochus, a tawny Moor all in white, and three or four followers accordingly, with Portia, Nerissa, and their train. Flo. Cornets."

2. **burnish'd.** Collier suggested 'burning' as an emendation, and this reading appeared in the earlier editions of Hudson's Shakespeare.

7. "Red blood is a traditionary sign of courage. Thus, Macbeth calls one of his frightened soldiers a 'lily-liver'd' boy; again, in this play, cowards are said to have 'livers as white as milk'; and an effeminate and timorous man is termed a milksop." — Johnson. For the superlative, 'reddest,' see Abbott, § 10.

PORTIA. In terms of choice I am not solely led
By nice direction of a maiden's eyes;
Besides, the lottery of my destiny   15
Bars me the right of voluntary choosing:
But, if my father had not scanted me,
And hedg'd me by his wit, to yield myself
His wife who wins me by that means I told you,
Yourself, renowned Prince, then stood as fair   20
As any comer I have look'd on yet
For my affection.

MOROCCO.   Even for that I thank you:
Therefore, I pray you, lead me to the caskets,
To try my fortune. By this scimitar
That slew the Sophy, and a Persian prince   25
That won three fields of Sultan Solyman,
I would out-stare the sternest eyes that look,

18. wit   QqFf | will   Hanmer   27. out-stare Q1 | ore-stare   Q2Ff
(Theobald conj.).   Q3Q4.

14. Portia means that reason and judgment have a voice potential
in her thoughts of marriage. So in *Hamlet*, IV, iii, 4: "the dis-
tracted multitude, Who like not in their judgment, but their eyes."

18. wit: judgment, foresight. Theobald suggested 'will' as an
emendation, and this reading was adopted in previous editions of
Hudson's Shakespeare.

25. Sophy. From *The History of the Warres between the Turkes
and the Persians* (London, 1595), Shakespeare might have learned
that "Soffi and Sofito, an ancient word signifying a wise man . . .
is growen to be the common name of the Emperour of Persia."
Ismael Sophi is said to have been the founder of what was called
the Suffavian dynasty. The same potentate is twice referred to in
Twelfth Night (II, v, 198; III, iv, 307).

26. Sultan Solyman. The reference is doubtless to Solyman the
Magnificent, the greatest sultan of the sixteenth century, who led a
disastrous campaign against the Persians in 1535.

Outbrave the heart most daring on the earth,
Pluck the young sucking cubs from the she-bear,
Yea, mock the lion when he roars for prey,   30
To win the lady. But, alas the while !
If Hercules and Lichas play at dice
Which is the better man, the greater throw
May turn by fortune from the weaker hand :
So is Alcides beaten by his rage ;   35
And so may I, blind fortune leading me,
Miss that which one unworthier may attain,
And die with grieving.

PORTIA.   You must take your chance ;
And either not attempt to choose at all,
Or swear, before you choose, if you choose wrong   40
Never to speak to lady afterward
In way of marriage : therefore be advis'd.

MOROCCO. Nor will not. Come, bring me unto my
      chance.

31. **the lady** | thee, lady Rowe   35. **rage** QqFf | page Theobald.
QqFf.

31. **alas the while.** An imprecation upon contemporary conditions
like " Woe the while ! " " Woe worth the day ! "

32–33. If they try the question of which is the braver man by a
game of dice. The story of Lichas and his bringing to Hercules the
" shirt bestained with the blood of Nessus " is found in Ovid's
Metamorphoses, IX. Hercules was a descendant of Alcæus, and so
is called, in the Greek idiom, Alcides, in l. 35. See also III, ii, 55.

35. **rage.** Almost all modern editors have accepted Theobald's
emendation, 'page.' But the text as it stands is more poetical and
Shakespearian. For an ingenious defense of the Folio reading see
Porter and Clarke's 'First Folio' edition of the play.

42. **advis'd.** " Therefore be not precipitant ; consider well what
you are to do. 'Advis'd' is the word opposite to 'rash.' " — Johnson.

43. **Nor . . . not.** See note, p. 15, l. 24.

PORTIA. First, forward to the temple : after dinner
Your hazard shall be made.

MOROCCO.   Good fortune then !   45
To make me blest or cursed'st among men.

[*Cornets, and exeunt*]

SCENE II. *Venice. A street*

Enter LAUNCELOT

LAUNCELOT. Certainly my conscience will serve me to
run from this Jew my master. The fiend is at mine elbow,
and tempts me, saying to me, 'Gobbo, Launcelot Gobbo,
good Launcelot,' or 'good Gobbo,' or 'good Launcelot
Gobbo, use your legs, take the start, run away.' My conscience says, 'No; take heed, honest Launcelot; take
heed, honest Gobbo,' or, as aforesaid, 'honest Launcelot
Gobbo; do not run; scorn running with thy heels.' Well,

Enter LAUNCELOT | Enter Laun-
celot alone Rowe | Enter the Clowne
alone QqFf.

3. **tempts** QqF₁F₂ | attempts F₃
F₄. — **Gobbo** Q₁ | Iobbe Q₂F₁ | Job
F₃.

44. temple. Keightley wished to substitute 'table,' but possibly
Portia's command to the Prince is to go to the church to take the
oath mentioned just before, and described more particularly in the
ninth scene of this act. Bibles were not kept in private houses in
Shakespeare's time; and such an oath had to be taken on the Bible.

46. The force of the superlative in 'cursed'st' retroacts on 'blest';
so that the sense is 'most blest or most cursed.' So in *Measure for
Measure*, IV, vi, 13, "The generous and gravest citizens."

8. To scorn a thing with the heels appears to have been an old
phrase for spurning or kicking at a thing. Shakespeare has the
phrase again in *Much Ado About Nothing*, III, iv, 50. Launcelot
seems to be in chase of a quibble between the heels as used in
kicking, and the heels as used in running.

the most courageous fiend bids me pack : ' Via ! ' says the
fiend ; 'away !' says the fiend ; ' for the heavens, rouse up
a brave mind,' says the fiend, ' and run.' Well, my conscience, hanging about the neck of my heart, says very wisely
to me, ' My honest friend Launcelot, being an honest man's
son,' — or rather an honest woman's son ; for, indeed, my
father did something smack, something grow to, he had a
kind of taste ; — well, my conscience says, ' Launcelot,
budge not.' ' Budge,' says the fiend. ' Budge not,' says
my conscience. ' Conscience,' say I, ' you counsel well' ;
' Fiend,' say I, ' you counsel well ' : to be ruled by my conscience, I should stay with the Jew my master, who, God
bless the mark, is a kind of devil ; and, to run away from

---

9. **Via** Rowe | fia QqFf.   19. **well** Q2Ff | ill Q1.

9. **Via** : away ! go ahead ! An Italian exclamation of encourage-
ment, sometimes of impatience, used in Elizabethan London by
teamsters and watermen.

10. **for the heavens.** A petty oath. To make the fiend conjure
Launcelot to do a thing for heaven's sake, is a bit of that "acute
nonsense " which Barrow makes a species of wit.

15. **something grow to.** "A household phrase applied to milk when
burnt to the bottom of the saucepan, and thence acquiring an unpleasant taste." — Clar. This expression, which suggests dishonesty, is
still in common use in country districts in Scotland and the North
of England.

20–21. **God bless the mark.** Like ' God save the mark,' an apologetic phrase. How these phrases grew into such use or acquired such
a meaning is not very clear. Bible expressions such as " The Lord set
a mark on Cain," " set a mark on the foreheads of the men," and
the many similar phrases in the Apocalypse, may have had their
influence. Certain congenital marks on the person were regarded as
ominous or ill-boding. So in *A Midsummer Night's Dream*, V, i,
418. " Never mole, hare lip, nor scar, Nor mark prodigious." And
so the phrases may have meant, " May God avert the evil omen ! "
or, " May God render the token auspicious ! "

the Jew, I should be ruled by the fiend, who, saving your
reverence, is the devil himself. Certainly the Jew is the
very devil incarnal; and, in my conscience, my conscience
is but a kind of hard conscience, to offer to counsel me to
stay with the Jew. The fiend gives the more friendly counsel: I will run, fiend; my heels are at your commandment;
I will run.   28

Enter OLD GOBBO, *with a basket*

GOBBO. Master young man, you, I pray you, which is
the way to master Jew's?   30

LAUNCELOT. [*Aside*] O heavens, this is my true-begotten
father! who, being more than sand-blind, high-gravel-blind,
knows me not: I will try confusions with him.

GOBBO. Master young gentleman, I pray you, which is
the way to master Jew's?   35

---

24. incarnal Q1 | incarnation Q2   27-28. commandment Q2Ff | com-
Ff.   mand Q1.

22–23. **saving your reverence.** Another apologetic expression. This
phrase usually introduced something coarse or profane; it is like
the modern "If you will allow me to say so."

24. **incarnal.** The Folios read 'incarnation,' but the First Quarto
reading, adopted in the text, is the more delicious Gobboism; as the
Folio 'commandment' in l. 27 is for the same reason preferable to
the First Quarto 'command.'

32. **sand-blind.** Launcelot's degrees of comparison — sand-blind,
high-gravel-blind, stone-blind! 'Sand,' probably a popular corruption
of Anglo-Saxon *sám*, half. Of course, Launcelot makes it the turn-
ing-point of a quibble.

33. **try confusions.** To 'try conclusions' is the old phrase for to
'try experiments.' It is not quite clear whether Launcelot's 'confusions' is a blunder for 'conclusions,' or whether it is an intentional
parody on the old phrase, by way of joke.

LAUNCELOT. Turn up on your right hand at the next turning, but, at the next turning of all, on your left; marry, at the very next turning, turn of no hand, but turn down indirectly to the Jew's house.   39

GOBBO. By God's sonties, 't will be a hard way to hit. Can you tell me whether one Launcelot, that dwells with him, dwell with him or no?   42

LAUNCELOT. Talk you of young Master Launcelot? — [*Aside*] Mark me now; now will I raise the waters. — Talk you of young Master Launcelot?   45

GOBBO. No master, sir, but a poor man's son : his father, though I say 't, is an honest exceeding poor man, and, God be thank'd, well to live.   48

36. **up on** Qq | upon Ff.   39. **to** Ff | unto Q1.

37. **marry.** Continually used as a colloquial intensive, having the force of 'verily,' 'indeed,' or 'forsooth': like the Latin *hercule* and *edepol.* It grew from a custom of swearing by the Virgin Mary.

40. **sonties.** Most likely a corruption either of 'saints' or of 'sanctity.' *Saunctes* is an old form of 'saints,' and a pronunciation very similar to that suggested in the text is still to be heard in Scotland.

44. **raise the waters:** come it over him, have some sport with him. Cf. the colloquial expression, "get a rise out of one." The explanation, "raise the waters in old Gobbo's eyes," seems strained and out of place, though ll. 59–66 may seem to favor it.

46. **master.** This word formerly meant something as a title of respect. "Whosoever studieth the laws of the realm, who studieth in the universities, who professeth liberal sciences ; and, to be short, who can live idly, and without manual labour, and will bear the port, charge, and countenance of a gentleman, he shall be called 'master.'" — *The Commonwealth of England,* 1612. Old Gobbo shrinks from giving his son the title, though he keeps calling him 'master,' not knowing who he is.

48. **well to live.** While this expression may mean 'sure of a long life,' the common use of the phrase and the spirit of the passage rather suggest 'well to do.' The old man is thus humorously made to contradict himself.

LAUNCELOT. Well, let his father be what a will, we talk
of young Master Launcelot.   50

GOBBO. Your worship's friend, and Launcelot, sir.

LAUNCELOT. But, I pray you, ergo, old man, ergo, I
beseech you, talk you of young Master Launcelot?

GOBBO. Of Launcelot, an't please your mastership.   54

LAUNCELOT. Ergo, Master Launcelot. Talk not of Master Launcelot, father ; for the young gentleman — according
to Fates and Destinies, and such odd sayings, the Sisters
Three, and such branches of learning — is, indeed, deceas'd ;
or, as you would say in plain terms, gone to heaven.   59

GOBBO. Marry, God forbid ! the boy was the very staff
of my age, my very prop.

LAUNCELOT. [*Aside*] Do I look like a cudgel or a hovel-
post, a staff or a prop ? — Do you know me, father?   63

GOBBO. Alack the day, I know you not, young gentleman : but, I pray you, tell me, is my boy — God rest his
soul ! — alive or dead?

LAUNCELOT. Do you not know me, father?   67

GOBBO. Alack, sir, I am sand-blind ; I know you not.

LAUNCELOT. Nay, indeed, if you had your eyes, you
might fail of the knowing me : it is a wise father that knows

51. sir Qq | omitted in Ff.

49. a : he. For Chaucer's use of 'a,' see Kittredge's *Troilus*, p. 152.
52. ergo : therefore. Schmidt catalogues Launcelot's foreign words.
63. Do you know me. Dyce thought a 'not' necessary here — a
suggestion adopted in early editions of Hudson's Shakespeare.
67. It was customary for young people to address any old man or
woman as father or mother. Hence old Gobbo does not recognize his
son on being called father by him. So, in *King Lear*, Edgar, while
leading the eyeless Gloucester, addresses him repeatedly as 'father,'
without stirring any suspicion of the relationship between them.

his own child. Well, old man, I will tell you news of your
son : give me your blessing. Truth will come to light ;
murder cannot be hid long, — a man's son may ; but, in
the end, truth will out.   74

GOBBO. Pray you, sir, stand up : I am sure you are not
Launcelot, my boy.

LAUNCELOT. Pray you, let 's have no more fooling about
it, but give me your blessing : I am Launcelot, your boy
that was, your son that is, your child that shall be.   79

GOBBO. I cannot think you are my son.

LAUNCELOT. I know not what I shall think of that : but
I am Launcelot, the Jew's man ; and I am sure Margery
your wife is my mother.   83

GOBBO. Her name is Margery, indeed : I 'll be sworn, if
thou be Launcelot, thou art mine own flesh and blood. Lord
worshipp'd might he be ! what a beard hast thou got ! thou
hast got more hair on thy chin than Dobbin my fill-horse
has on his tail.   88

LAUNCELOT. It should seem, then, that Dobbin's tail
grows backward : I am sure he had more hair of his tail
than I have of my face, when I last saw him.

73-74. in the end Q2Ff | at the length Q1.

72. give me your blessing. After 'blessing' Dyce inserted the
direction, "Kneels, with his back to Gobbo." Quartos and Folios
have no such direction, but Gobbo's amusing mistake about hair and
beard, ll. 86–87, shows that when Launcelot knelt to receive the
blessing he did so with his back to his father.

79. Launcelot probably means "your child that was, your boy
that is, your son that shall be."

85. thou. As soon as Gobbo recognizes his son, the 'you' of respect
is changed to the 'thou' of familiarity.

87. fill-horse : a horse that works in shafts. 'Fill' is a dialect
form of 'thill.'

GOBBO. Lord, how art thou chang'd! How dost thou
and thy master agree? I have brought him a present.
How 'gree you now?   94

LAUNCELOT. Well, well; but, for mine own part, as I
have set up my rest to run away, so I will not rest till I
have run some ground. My master's a very Jew: give him
a present! give him a halter: I am famish'd in his service;
you may tell every finger I have with my ribs. Father, I am
glad you are come: give me your present to one Master
Bassanio, who, indeed, gives rare new liveries: if I serve
not him, I will run as far as God has any ground. — O rare
fortune! here comes the man: — to him, father; for I am
a Jew, if I serve the Jew any longer.   104

Enter BASSANIO, *with* LEONARDO *and other followers*

BASSANIO. You may do so; but let it be so hasted, that
supper be ready at the farthest by five of the clock. See
these letters deliver'd; put the liveries to making; and
desire Gratiano to come anon to my lodging.   108

[*Exit a* Servant]

LAUNCELOT. To him, father.

GOBBO. God bless your worship!

BASSANIO. Gramercy! wouldst thou aught with me? 111

96. **set up my rest.** A phrase in frequent use for making up one's
mind. Said to be taken from the old game of primero, where it
meant determination to stand upon the cards you held in your hand.

102. A humorous expression from any one, but with additional
edge and flavor from a Venetian. In Venice proper it was not easy
to find ground enough to run away upon.

111. **Gramercy**: many thanks. Fr. *grand merci*. But the word is
often used as an interjection of surprise.

GOBBO. Here's my son, sir, a poor boy, —   112

LAUNCELOT. Not a poor boy, sir, but the rich Jew's man;
that would, sir, — as my father shall specify, —

GOBBO. He hath a great infection, sir, as one would say,
to serve, —   116

LAUNCELOT. Indeed, the short and the long is, I serve
the Jew, and have a desire, — as my father shall specify, —

GOBBO. His master and he — saving your worship's reverence — are scarce cater-cousins, —   120

LAUNCELOT. To be brief, the very truth is, that the Jew
having done me wrong doth cause me, — as my father, being,
I hope, an old man, shall frutify unto you, —

GOBBO. I have here a dish of doves that I would bestow
upon your worship; and my suit is, —   125

LAUNCELOT. In very brief, the suit is impertinent to myself, as your worship shall know by this honest old man; and,
though I say it, though old man, yet, poor man, my father.

BASSANIO. One speak for both. — What would you?

115. **infection.** A Gobboism for 'affection,' i.e. 'desire.'

120. **cater-cousins.** Attempts have been made in recent years to
connect the word 'cater' etymologically with 'cate,' food, and with
quêteur. Johnson's suggestion that it is from *quatre*, which would
make 'cater-cousins' mean 'fourth cousins,' is certainly wrong. Old
Gobbo's meaning is clear: his son and Shylock are not on friendly
terms. His expression carries an apology with it.

123. **frutify.** A Gobboism for 'fructify,' which appears to have
been a sort of cant term for 'holding forth' (in speech). It has
been suggested that 'frutify' may balance 'specify' ('spicify,' spice
and fruit), l. 114.

124. "A present thus given, and in our days too, and of doves, is
not uncommon in Italy. I myself have partaken there, with due
relish, in memory of poor old Gobbo, of a dish of doves, presented
by the father of a servant." — C. A. BROWN.

LAUNCELOT. Serve you, sir.   130

GOBBO. That is the very defect of the matter, sir.

BASSANIO. I know thee well; thou hast obtain'd thy suit:
Shylock thy master spoke with me this day,
And hath preferr'd thee, if it be preferment
To leave a rich Jew's service, to become   135
The follower of so poor a gentleman.

LAUNCELOT. The old proverb is very well parted between
my master Shylock and you, sir: you have the grace of God,
sir, and he hath enough.   139

BASSANIO. Thou speak'st it well. — Go, father, with thy
son. —
Take leave of thy old master, and inquire
My lodging out.   Give him a livery
More guarded than his fellows': see it done.   143

LAUNCELOT. Father, in. — I cannot get a service, no; I
have ne'er a tongue in my head. — Well, if any man in
Italy have a fairer table! which doth offer to swear upon a

---

134. 'To prefer' is, in Elizabethan English, 'to recommend' as
well as 'to promote.' Bassanio plays upon the two senses of the word.

137. **The old proverb.**   Clark and Wright cite here, "The grace of
God is geir enough" (*Ray's Proverbs*, 1670).   The use of 'gear' in
l. 153 of this scene may strengthen this identification of the proverb.

142. After 'out' some editions introduce the direction, 'To his
followers.'

143. **guarded**: trimmed with braid.   See Murray.

145. After 'Well' some editions introduce the direction, 'Looking on his palm.'

145–146. Launcelot, applauding himself for his success with
Bassanio, and looking into the palm of his hand, which by fortune-
tellers is called the 'table,' breaks out into reflection: "Well, if any
man in Italy have a fairer table, which not only promises, but offers
to swear upon a book, that I shall have good fortune."

book, I shall have good fortune! Go to; here's a simple
line of life! here's a small trifle of wives: alas! fifteen
wives is nothing! aleven widows and nine maids is a simple
coming-in for one man; and then to 'scape drowning thrice,
and to be in peril of my life with the edge of a feather-bed,
— here are simple 'scapes! Well, if Fortune be a woman,
she's a good wench for this gear. — Father, come; I'll take
my leave of the Jew in the twinkling of an eye.   154

[*Exeunt* LAUNCELOT *and* OLD GOBBO]

BASSANIO. I pray thee, good Leonardo, think on this:
These things being bought and orderly bestow'd,
Return in haste, for I do feast to-night
My best-esteem'd acquaintance: hie thee, go.   158

LEONARDO. My best endeavours shall be done herein.

---

154. of an eye Q1 | omitted in Q2Ff.

147–148. The line in the palm passing round the ball of the thumb,
technically known as the Mount of Venus, was called by sixteenth
century palmists, the line of life; that which runs from the forefinger
below the other fingers to the side of the hand, was the line of fortune. "Long and deep lines from the Mount of Venus towards the
line of life signifieth so many wives . . . These lines, visible and
deep, so many wives the party shall have." — Saunders, *Chiromancie*.
Launcelot, like Subtle in Ben Jonson's *The Alchemist* (cf. the speech
beginning 'The thumb, in chiromancy, we give Venus'), was an adept
in the art of chiromancy, which in his time had its learned profes-
sors and practitioners no less than astrology. "A simple line of life"
written in the palm was cause of exultation to wiser ones than young
Gobbo, though 'simple' here is doubtless ironical, and balances the
'simple' in l. 149.

149. aleven. "A vulgarism (and archaism) for eleven." — Dyce.
The expression appears in Q2 and F1 as 'a leven,' suggesting the
analogy of 'a dozen.'

151. the edge of a feather-bed. This is a humorous variation of the
phrase, "the edge of the sword."

Enter GRATIANO

GRATIANO. Where is your master?

LEONARDO.   Yonder, sir, he walks.

                                                [Exit]

GRATIANO. Signior Bassanio, —

BASSANIO. Gratiano !   162

GRATIANO. I have a suit to you.

BASSANIO.   You have obtain'd it.

GRATIANO. You must not deny me : I must go with you
to Belmont.   165

BASSANIO. Why, then you must. But hear thee, Gratiano :
Thou art too wild, too rude, and bold of voice, —
Parts that become thee happily enough,
And in such eyes as ours appear not faults ;
But where thou art not known, why, there they show   170
Something too liberal. Pray thee, take pain
To allay with some cold drops of modesty
Thy skipping spirit ; lest, through thy wild behaviour,
I be misconstru'd in the place I go to,
And lose my hopes.

GRATIANO.   Signior Bassanio, hear me :   175
If I do not put on a sober habit,

---

160. Scene III Pope.
170. thou art Qq | they are Ff.
173. lest Q1F4 | least Q2F1.

174. **misconstru'd** | misconstred
Qq | misconsterd F1.
175. **lose** Q1 | loose Q2Ff.

164. Hanmer and Capell inserted 'Nay' at the beginning of
Gratiano's speech and printed it as verse — an arrangement followed
in the earlier editions of Hudson's Shakespeare.

166. hear thee. See Abbott, § 212. Professor Gummere declares
Abbott's explanation to be "certainly wrong," and refers to "the
excellent discussion of the substitution of 'thee' for 'thou'" given
by Jespersen in *Progress in Language*.

176. habit: demeanor.

Talk with respect, and swear but now and then,
Wear prayer-books in my pocket, look demurely;
Nay more, while grace is saying, hood mine eyes
Thus with my hat, and sigh, and say 'amen';   180
Use all the observance of civility,
Like one well studied in a sad ostent
To please his grandam, never trust me more.

    BASSANIO. Well, we shall see your bearing.   184

    GRATIANO. Nay, but I bar to-night: you shall not gage me
By what we do to-night.

    BASSANIO.   No, that were pity:
I would entreat you rather to put on
Your boldest suit of mirth, for we have friends
That purpose merriment. But fare you well:
I have some business.   190

    GRATIANO. And I must to Lorenzo and the rest:
But we will visit you at supper-time.   [*Exeunt*]

SCENE III. *The same. A room in* SHYLOCK'S *house*

Enter JESSICA *and* LAUNCELOT

    JESSICA. I am sorry thou wilt leave my father so:
Our house is hell; and thou, a merry devil,

SCENE III Capell I Scene IV Pope. | Enter Jessica and the Clown Qq
Enter JESSICA *and* LAUNCELOT   Ff.

180. People of rank used to keep their hats on while eating
dinner. While grace was being said they were expected to take the
hat off and hold it over the eyes.
181. **civility**: good breeding. "Civilization, refinement." — Clar.
182. **sad ostent**: serious appearance. "Show of staid . . . behaviour." — Johnson.

Didst rob it of some taste of tediousness.
But fare thee well; there is a ducat for thee:
And, Launcelot, soon at supper shalt thou see   5
Lorenzo, who is thy new master's guest:
Give him this letter; do it secretly;
And so farewell! I would not have my father
See me in talk with thee.   9

LAUNCELOT. Adieu! tears exhibit my tongue. Most
beautiful pagan, most sweet Jew! if a Christian do not
play the knave and get thee, I am much deceiv'd. But,
adieu: these foolish drops do something drown my manly
spirit: adieu.   14

JESSICA. Farewell, good Launcelot. — [*Exit* LAUNCELOT]
Alack, what heinous sin is it in me
To be asham'd to be my father's child!
But though I am a daughter to his blood,
I am not to his manners. O Lorenzo,
If thou keep promise, I shall end this strife,   20
Become a Christian, and thy loving wife!   [*Exit*]

---

9. **me in talk** Qq | me talk Ff.   13. **something** Qq | somewhat Ff.
11. **do** QqF₁ | did F₂F₃F₄.

5. **soon at.** Here 'soon' has the effect of emphasis, as in *The Comedy of Errors*, I, ii, 26; III, ii, 179; *Richard III*, IV, iii, 31.

10. **exhibit.** Most probably a Gobboism for 'inhibit' or as Halliwell suggested, 'prohibit.' But the meaning may be, as Eccles put it: "My tears express what my tongue should, if sorrow would permit it."

11. The spirit of this scene, Jessica's reference to Lorenzo when giving Launcelot the letter, and the closing words of her soliloquy, sufficiently justify the reading of all the Quartos and the First Folio.

16. **alack.** See Skeat for an interesting note as to derivation.

SCENE IV. *The same. A street*

Enter GRATIANO, LORENZO, SALARINO, *and* SALANIO

LORENZO. Nay, we will slink away in supper-time,
Disguise us at my lodging, and return
All in an hour.

GRATIANO. We have not made good preparation.

SALARINO. We have not spoke us yet of torch-bearers. 5

SALANIO. 'T is vile, unless it may be quaintly order'd,
And better in my mind not undertook.

LORENZO. 'T is now but four o'clock : we have two hours
To furnish us. —

Enter LAUNCELOT, *with a letter*

                    Friend Launcelot, what's the news?

LAUNCELOT. And it shall please you to break up this, it
shall seem to signify.   11

LORENZO. I know the hand : in faith, 't is a fair hand ;
And whiter than the paper it writ on
Is the fair hand that writ.

GRATIANO.   Love-news, in faith.

LAUNCELOT. By your leave, sir.   15

SCENE IV Capell | Scene V Pope.   5. us QqF$_1$F$_2$F$_3$ | as F$_4$.
2–3. Printed as prose QqFf.   10–11. it shall Qq | shall it F$_1$.

5. **us.** Ethical dative, if not a misprint for 'as.' The line means,
we have not yet bespoken torch-bearers.

6. **quaintly**: noticeably — not derived from *comptus*, but, through
Old Fr. *coint*, from *cognitus*, and connotes the idea of attracting
attention.

10. **And.** See note, p. 19, l. 80. — **break up** : break the seal of.

13. **paper it writ.** Hanmer suggested the emendation 'paper that
it writ,' and this reading was adopted in early editions of Hudson's
Shakespeare.

LORENZO. Whither goest thou?

LAUNCELOT. Marry, sir, to bid my old master the Jew to
sup to-night with my new master the Christian.

LORENZO. Hold here, take this : tell gentle Jessica
I will not fail her; speak it privately;   20
Go. — Gentlemen,   [*Exit* LAUNCELOT]
Will you prepare you for this masque to-night?
I am provided of a torch-bearer.

SALARINO. Ay, marry, I 'll be gone about it straight.

SALANIO. And so will I.

LORENZO.   Meet me and Gratiano   25
At Gratiano's lodging some hour hence.

SALARINO. 'T is good we do so.

                        [*Exeunt* SALARINO *and* SALANIO]

GRATIANO. Was not that letter from fair Jessica?

LORENZO. I must needs tell thee all : She hath directed
How I shall take her from her father's house ;   30
What gold and jewels she is furnish'd with ;
What page's suit she hath in readiness.
If e'er the Jew her father come to heaven,
It will be for his gentle daughter's sake ;
And never dare misfortune cross her foot,   35
Unless she do it under this excuse,
That she is issue to a faithless Jew.
Come, go with me : peruse this as thou goest.
Fair Jessica shall be my torch-bearer.   [*Exeunt*]

23. **provided of.** "We still retain 'of' with verbs of construction and
adjectives of fulness; but the Elizabethans retained 'of' with verbs of
fulness also." — Abbott, § 171. Cf. V, i, 297; *Macbeth*, I, ii, 13; *Henry V*,
III, vii, 9. In Bacon's *The Advancement of Learning* we have : "He
is invested of a precedent disposition to conform himself thereunto."

37. **faithless** : unbelieving. Cf. "O faithless generation !" —
Mark, ix, 19.

SCENE V. *The same. Before* SHYLOCK'S *house*

Enter SHYLOCK *and* LAUNCELOT

SHYLOCK. Well, thou shalt see, thy eyes shall be thy judge,
The difference of old Shylock and Bassanio : —
What, Jessica ! — thou shalt not gormandize,
As thou hast done with me, — what, Jessica ! —
And sleep and snore, and rend apparel out. —   5
Why, Jessica, I say !

LAUNCELOT.   Why, Jessica !

SHYLOCK. Who bids thee call? I do not bid thee call.

LAUNCELOT. Your worship was wont to tell me I could
do nothing without bidding.

Enter JESSICA

JESSICA. Call you? what is your will?   10

SHYLOCK. I am bid forth to supper, Jessica :
There are my keys. — But wherefore should I go?
I am not bid for love ; they flatter me :
But yet I 'll go in hate, to feed upon
The prodigal Christian. — Jessica, my girl,   15
Look to my house. — I am right loth to go :
There is some ill a-brewing towards my rest,
For I did dream of money-bags to-night.

SCENE V Capell | Scene VI Pope.   8-9. Prose in Q1 | verse in Q2Ff.

14-15. In I, iii, 33, Shylock says, " I will not eat with you, drink
with you, nor pray with you." Did Shakespeare make a slip, or did
he mean to put the Jew at odds with himself out of hatred to the
Christian ? Cf. the oversight noted on p. 21, l. 114.

18. to-night : last night. See Abbott, § 190. Cf. *Julius Cæsar*, II, ii,
76 ; III, iii, 1. In l. 36 'to-night' is used in the modern sense.

LAUNCELOT. I beseech you, sir, go: my young master
doth expect your reproach.   20

SHYLOCK. So do I his.

LAUNCELOT. And they have conspir'd together, — I will
not say you shall see a masque; but if you do, then it was
not for nothing that my nose fell a-bleeding on Black-
Monday last at six o'clock i' the morning, falling out that
year on Ash-Wednesday was four year in the afternoon.   26

SHYLOCK. What, are there masques? — Hear you me,
    Jessica:
Lock up my doors; and, when you hear the drum,
And the vile squealing of the wry-neck'd fife,
Clamber not you up to the casements then,   30
Nor thrust your head into the public street,
To gaze on Christian fools with varnish'd faces;

27. **you** omitted in Q1.   29. **squealing** Q2Ff | squeaking Q1.

20. **reproach.** A Gobboism for 'approach.' Shylock chooses to take
it in the sense of 'reproach.' And he expects Bassanio's reproach
through the bankruptcy of Antonio. This may have some bearing
on the question whether Shylock has any hand in getting up the
reports of Antonio's "losses at sea."

24–25. **Black-Monday**: Easter-Monday. The origin of the name is
thus explained by Stow: " In the 34th of Edward III, the 14th of
April, and the morrow after Easter-day, King Edward, with his host,
lay before the city of Paris: which day was full dark of mist and hail,
and so bitter cold, that many men died on their horses' backs with the
cold. Wherefore unto this day it hath been called the *Black Monday*."

29. **wry-neck'd fife.** There has been some dispute whether this
means the instrument or the musician. Boswell cited a passage
from Barnabe Rich's *Aphorisms*, 1618, which appears to settle the
matter: "A fife is a wry-neckt musician, for he always looks away
from his instrument."

32. **varnish'd faces.** This alludes probably to the painted masks,
but contains also an insinuation of duplicity, or double-facedness.

But stop my house's ears, — I mean my casements :
Let not the sound of shallow foppery enter
My sober house. — By Jacob's staff, I swear   35
I have no mind of feasting forth to-night :
But I will go. — Go you before me, sirrah ;
Say I will come.

LAUNCELOT. I will go before, sir. — Mistress, look out at
window for all this ;   40
                    There will come a Christian by,
                    Will be worth a Jewess' eye.   [*Exit*]

SHYLOCK. What says that fool of Hagar's offspring, ha ?

JESSICA. His words were, 'Farewell, mistress'; nothing else.

SHYLOCK. The patch is kind enough ; but a huge feeder,
Snail-slow in profit, and he sleeps by day   46
More than the wild-cat : drones hive not with me ;
Therefore I part with him ; and part with him

---

42. **Jewess'** Pope Camb | Jewes   46. **and he** Qq | but he F₁ | but
QqF₁F₂ | Jew's F₃F₄.   F₂F₃F₄ Rowe.

35. **Jacob's staff.** *Genesis*, xxxii, 10 ; *Hebrews*, xi, 21.

39–40. In Quartos and Folios this speech of Launcelot's is printed :

> I will go before sir.
> Mistress look out at window for all this.

Walker suggested the emendation, " I 'll go before you, sir," adopted
in previous editions of Hudson's Shakespeare.

42. Pope suggested 'Jewess'' as the reading here ; but the Quartos
and First Folio have 'Jewes,' which may mean either 'Jewess'' or
'Jew's.' The worth of a Jew's eye was the price with which the
Jews used to buy themselves off from mutilation. The expression
became proverbial, and was kept up after its original meaning was lost.

45. This use of 'patch' sprang from the motley or patched dress
worn by professional fools. Hence a general term of contempt. So
used in *A Midsummer Night's Dream*, III, ii, 9 ; *The Comedy of
Errors*, III, i, 32 ; III, i, 36, etc. Cf. 'cross-patch.'

To one that I would have him help to waste
His borrow'd purse. —Well, Jessica, go in :   50
Perhaps I will return immediately :
Do as I bid you; shut doors after you :
Fast bind, fast find, —
A proverb never stale in thrifty mind.   [*Exit*]

JESSICA.   Farewell ; and if my fortune be not crost,   55
I have a father, you a daughter, lost.   [*Exit*]

SCENE VI.   *The same*

Enter GRATIANO *and* SALARINO, *masqued*

GRATIANO.   This is the pent-house under which Lorenzo
Desir'd us to make stand.

SALARINO.   His hour is almost past.

GRATIANO.   And it is marvel he out-dwells his hour,
For lovers ever run before the clock.

SALARINO.   O, ten times faster Venus' pigeons fly   5
To seal love's bonds new-made than they are wont,
To keep obliged faith unforfeited !

GRATIANO.   That ever holds.   Who riseth from a feast
With that keen appetite that he sits down?
Where is the horse that doth untread again   10

52-53. One line in Q₂Ff.   2. **make stand** Qq | make a stand Ff.
SCENE VI Capell | Scene VII Pope.   6. **seal** Qq | steal Ff.

SCENE VI. In Halliwell, in Dyce, and in previous editions of Hudson's Shakespeare, there was no new scene here.

5. In classic fable Venus rode the air in a chariot drawn by
doves. Cf. *The Tempest*, IV, i, 94.

9. For the omission of the preposition in relative sentences, see
Abbott, § 394.

His tedious measures with the unbated fire
That he did pace them first? All things that are,
Are with more spirit chased than enjoy'd.
How like a younker or a prodigal
The scarfed bark puts from her native bay,   15
Hugg'd and embraced by the strumpet wind !
How like the prodigal doth she return,
With over-weather'd ribs, and ragged sails,
Lean, rent, and beggar'd by the strumpet wind !   19
    SALARINO. Here comes Lorenzo : more of this hereafter.

Enter LORENZO

    LORENZO. Sweet friends, your patience for my long abode ;
Not I, but my affairs, have made you wait :
When you shall please to play the thieves for wives,
I 'll watch as long for you then. Approach ;
Here dwells my father Jew. Ho ! who 's within?   25

Enter JESSICA, *above, in boy's clothes*

    JESSICA. Who are you? Tell me, for more certainty,
Albeit I 'll swear that I do know your tongue.
    LORENZO. Lorenzo, and thy love.
    JESSICA. Lorenzo, certain ; and my love, indeed ;
For who love I so much? And now who knows   30
But you, Lorenzo, whether I am yours?

---

14. **younker** Rowe | younger Qq   17. **the prodigal** Qq | a prodigal
| yonger F₁F₂.   Ff.

15. **scarfed** : decked with flags. Cf. *All 's Well that Ends Well*,
II, iii, 214.
21. **abode** : stay, delay. So in *Cymbeline*, I, vi, 53 : "My man's
abode where I did leave him."

LORENZO. Heaven and thy thoughts are witness that
    thou art.

JESSICA. Here, catch this casket; it is worth the pains.
I am glad 't is night, you do not look on me,
For I am much asham'd of my exchange :   35
But love is blind, and lovers cannot see
The pretty follies that themselves commit;
For, if they could, Cupid himself would blush
To see me thus transformed to a boy.

    LORENZO. Descend, for you must be my torch-bearer. 40

    JESSICA. What, must I hold a candle to my shames?
They in themselves, good sooth, are too too light.
Why, 't is an office of discovery, love ;
And I should be obscur'd.

    LORENZO.   So are you, sweet,
Even in the lovely garnish of a boy.   45
But come at once ;
For the close night doth play the runaway,
And we are stay'd for at Bassanio's feast.

    JESSICA. I will make fast the doors, and gild myself
With some more ducats, and be with you straight.   50

                         [*Exit above*]

GRATIANO. Now, by my hood, a Gentile, and no Jew.

44. are you Qq | you are Ff.   51. Gentile Q1Q3Q4F2F3F4 | gentle
50. more Ff | mo Q1Q2.   Q2F1.

35. **exchange** : change of dress. Referring to her masculine attire.
42. **light.** Used here punningly in a material and a moral sense.
43. A torch-bearer's office is to discover.
51. Gratiano is disguised with a mask, and in swearing by his hood
he implies a likening of himself to a hooded monk swearing by his
monastic character. There is also a play on the word 'Gentile,' which,
as Johnson pointed out, signifies both a heathen and one well-born.

LORENZO. Beshrew me but I love her heartily ;
For she is wise, if I can judge of her ;
And fair she is, if that mine eyes be true ;
And true she is, as she hath prov'd herself ;   55
And therefore, like herself, wise, fair, and true,
Shall she be placed in my constant soul.

Enter JESSICA, *below*

What, art thou come? — On, gentlemen ; away !
Our masquing mates by this time for us stay.
                    [*Exit, with* JESSICA *and* SALARINO]

Enter ANTONIO

ANTONIO. Who 's there?   60
GRATIANO. Signior Antonio !
ANTONIO. Fie, fie, Gratiano ! where are all the rest?
'T is nine o'clock ; our friends all stay for you.
No masque to-night : the wind is come about ;
Bassanio presently will go aboard :   65
I have sent twenty out to seek for you.
GRATIANO. I am glad on 't : I desire no more delight
Than to be under sail and gone to-night.   [*Exeunt*]

66. Omitted in Q1.   67-68. Given to Antonio in Q1.

52. **Beshrew me** : curse me. So Chaucer uses *shrewe* in this sense,
as in *The Nonne Preestes Tale :*

> " Nay than," quod he, " I shrewe us bothe two,
>   And first I shrewe my-self, bothe blood and bones."

After such an expression as 'beshrew me,' 'but' is not adversative.
but means 'if not.' See Abbott, § 126.
66. "The omission of a whole line here in Q1, and continuing
Gratiano's speech to Antonio, is an inexcusable defect." — Furness.

SCENE VII. *Belmont. A room in* PORTIA'S *house*

Flourish of cornets. Enter PORTIA, *with the* PRINCE OF
MOROCCO, *and their trains*

PORTIA. Go draw aside the curtains, and discover
The several caskets to this noble prince. —
Now make your choice.

MOROCCO. The first, of gold, who this inscription bears,
'Who chooseth me shall gain what many men desire;'   5
The second, silver, which this promise carries,
'Who chooseth me shall get as much as he deserves;'
This third, dull lead, with warning all as blunt,
'Who chooseth me must give and hazard all he hath.'
How shall I know if I do choose the right?   10

PORTIA. The one of them contains my picture, prince:
If you choose that, then I am yours withal.

MOROCCO. Some god direct my judgment! Let me see;
I will survey the inscriptions back again.
What says this leaden casket?   15
'Who chooseth me must give and hazard all he hath.'
Must give, — for what? for lead? hazard for lead?
This casket threatens. Men that hazard all
Do it in hope of fair advantages:
A golden mind stoops not to shows of dross;   20
I 'll then nor give nor hazard aught for lead.

SCENE VII Capell | Scene   10. This line is repeated in F₁F₂.
VIII Pope | Scene VI Halliwell.   18. threatens. Men Rowe | threatens
    5. many Qq | omitted in Ff.   men QqFf.

4. who. Pope substituted 'which.' But 'who' and 'which' were
interchangeable in the sixteenth century. See Abbott, § 264.

What says the silver with her virgin hue?
'Who chooseth me shall get as much as he deserves.'
As much as he deserves! Pause there, Morocco,
And weigh thy value with an even hand :   25
If thou be'st rated by thy estimation,
Thou dost deserve enough ; and yet enough
May not extend so far as to the lady :
And yet to be afeard of my deserving
Were but a weak disabling of myself.   30
As much as I deserve ! Why, that 's the lady :
I do in birth deserve her, and in fortunes,
In graces, and in qualities of breeding ;
But more than these, in love I do deserve.
What if I stray'd no further, but chose here?   35
Let 's see once more this saying grav'd in gold :
'Who chooseth me shall gain what many men desire.'
Why, that 's the lady ; all the world desires her :
From the four corners of the earth they come,
To kiss this shrine, this mortal breathing saint :   40

35. further | farther QqFf.   mortal-breathing Dyce Walker
40. mortal breathing QqFf | Camb.

22. **virgin.** An allusion to the silver light of the moon, or rather
to the virgin Diana, who was the moon goddess of old mythology.

26. **be'st.** See Abbott, § 298.

30. **disabling** : disparagement. Cf. Montrose's *My Dear and Only
Love :*

> He either fears his fate too much
>   Or his deserts are small,
> That dares not put it to the touch
>   To gain or lose it all.

40. Christians often made long prilgrimages to kiss the shrine of
a saint. And Portia, enshrining so much excellence, is compared to
such a shrine. 'Shrine,' however, was sometimes used for 'statue,'
and so it may be here. Cf. *Cymbeline*, V, v, 164.

The Hyrcanian deserts and the vasty wilds
Of wide Arabia are as throughfares now
For princes to come view fair Portia :
The watery kingdom, whose ambitious head
Spits in the face of heaven, is no bar   45
To stop the foreign spirits ; but they come,
As o'er a brook, to see fair Portia.
One of these three contains her heavenly picture.
Is 't like that lead contains her?   'T were damnation
To think so base a thought : it were too gross   50
To rib her cerecloth in the obscure grave.
Or shall I think in silver she 's immur'd,
Being ten times undervalu'd to tried gold?
O sinful thought ! Never so rich a gem
Was set in worse than gold. They have in England   55
A coin that bears the figure of an angel
Stamped in gold, but that 's insculp'd upon ;
But here an angel in a golden bed
Lies all within. — Deliver me the key :
Here do I choose, and thrive I as I may !   60

---

41. **vasty** Q1 | vaste F1F2 | vast F3F4.   45. **spits** Rowe | spets QqFf.

41. **Hyrcanian deserts.** A wilderness of indefinite extent south
of the Caspian Sea, often mentioned in old writers as a habitat of
tigers. Cf. *Macbeth*, III, iv, 101 ; *Hamlet*, II, ii, 472.

51. Lead were unworthy to inclose even her cerements, or her
shroud.

53. This is said to have been just the ratio of silver and gold
toward the close of Elizabeth's reign.

56. The 'angel' was so called from its having on one side a figure
of Michael piercing the dragon. It is said to have been worth about
ten shillings. Shakespeare has other punning allusions to it ; as in
The Merry Wives of Windsor, I, iii, 59.

PORTIA. There, take it, prince ; and if my form lie there,
Then I am yours.   [*He unlocks the casket*]

MOROCCO.   O hell ! what have we here?
A carrion Death, within whose empty eye
There is a written scroll ! I 'll read the writing.

[*Reads*] All that glisters is not gold ;   65
          Often have you heard that told :
          Many a man his life hath sold
          But my outside to behold :
          Gilded timber do worms infold.
          Had you been as wise as bold,   70
          Young in limbs, in judgment old,
          Your answer had not been inscroll'd :
          Fare you well ; your suit is cold.

     Cold, indeed, and labour lost ;
       Then, farewell, heat, and welcome, frost !   75
Portia, adieu. I have too griev'd a heart
To take a tedious leave : thus losers part.
                    [*Exit, with his train. Flourish of cornets*]
     PORTIA. A gentle riddance. — Draw the curtains ; go :
Let all of his complexion choose me so.   [*Exeunt*]

62-64. **O hell! what . . . a written scroll** | printed as two lines in QqFf. — **I 'll read the writing** QqF1 | omitted in F2F3F4. — No stage directions in QqFf.

69. **timber do** QqFf | tombs do Capell (Johnson conj.).

77. *Flourish of cornets* transferred here from next scene by editors of Camb.

63. **A carrion Death**: a skull from which the flesh has decayed.

69. **timber.** "'Timber' is here a plural noun, and the redundant syllable is no sufficient reason for adopting Johnson's plausible alteration." — Halliwell.

77. **part**: depart. 'Depart' was also used for 'part,' ". . . as in the Marriage Service 'till death us do part' is a corruption of 'till death us depart.'" — Clar.

SCENE VIII. *Venice. A street*

Enter SALARINO *and* SALANIO

SALARINO. Why, man, I saw Bassanio under sail :
With him is Gratiano gone along ;
And in their ship I 'm sure Lorenzo is not.

SALANIO. The villain Jew with outcries rais'd the Duke ;
Who went with him to search Bassanio's ship.   5

SALARINO. He came too late, the ship was under sail ;
But there the Duke was given to understand
That in a gondola were seen together
Lorenzo and his amorous Jessica :
Besides, Antonio certified the Duke   10
They were not with Bassanio in his ship.

SALANIO. I never heard a passion so confus'd,
So strange, outrageous, and so variable,
As the dog Jew did utter in the streets :
'My daughter ! O my ducats ! O my daughter !   15
Fled with a Christian ! O my Christian ducats ! ·
Justice ! the law ! my ducats, and my daughter !
A sealed bag, two sealed bags of ducats,
Of double ducats, stolen from me by my daughter !
And jewels, two stones, two rich and precious stones,   20
Stolen by my daughter ! Justice ! find the girl !
She hath the stones upon her, and the ducats !'

SCENE VIII Capell | Scene IX
Pope | Scene VII Dyce.
6. **came** Qq | comes Ff.

8. gondola | Gondylo Qq | Gon-
dilo Ff | Gondalo Rowe.

8. In Shakespeare's time Venice was the common resort of all
who went abroad to see the world. " ' To have swum in a gondola '
was a phrase almost proverbial for having travelled." — Clar.

SALARINO. Why, all the boys in Venice follow him,
Crying, his stones, his daughter, and his ducats.

SALANIO. Let good Antonio look he keep his day,   25
Or he shall pay for this.

SALARINO.   Marry, well remember'd.
I reason'd with a Frenchman yesterday,
Who told me, in the narrow seas that part
The French and English, there miscarried
A vessel of our country richly fraught :   30
I thought upon Antonio when he told me ;
And wish'd in silence that it were not his.

SALANIO. You were best to tell Antonio what you hear ;
Yet do not suddenly, for it may grieve him.

SALARINO. A kinder gentleman treads not the earth.   35
I saw Bassanio and Antonio part :
Bassanio told him he would make some speed
Of his return : he answer'd, 'Do not so ;
Slubber not business for my sake, Bassanio,
But stay the very riping of the time ;   40
And for the Jew's bond which he hath of me,
Let it not enter in your mind of love :

39. Slubber Q₁Ff | slumber Q₂Q₃Q₄.

27. In Shakespeare the usual sense of 'to reason' is 'to talk' or
'to converse.' Cf. I, ii, 19; *Coriolanus*, I, ix, 58; IV, vi, 51.

33. You were best: it were best for you. 'You' here is dative, the
construction being impersonal. Cf. *King Lear*, I, iv, 109.

39. Here the word 'slubber' means 'to slur over,' as in Fuller's
The Worthies of England: " Slightly slubbering it over, doing something for show, and nothing to purpose." But the original meaning
is 'to soil' or 'to obscure,' as in *Othello*, I, iii, 227.

42. mind of love: loving mind, or mind full of love. So Shakespeare uses 'mind of honour' for 'honourable mind.'

Be merry; and employ your chiefest thoughts
To courtship, and such fair ostents of love
As shall conveniently become you there : '   45
And even there, his eye being big with tears,
Turning his face, he put his hand behind him,
And with affection wondrous sensible
He wrung Bassanio's hand ; and so they parted.

SALANIO.   I think he only loves the world for him.   50
I pray thee, let us go and find him out,
And quicken his embraced heaviness
With some delight or other.

SALARINO.   Do we so.   [*Exeunt*]

SCENE IX.   *Belmont.   A room in* PORTIA'S *house*

Enter NERISSA, *with a* Servitor

NERISSA.   Quick, quick, I pray thee ; draw the curtain
      straight :
The Prince of Arragon hath ta'en his oath,
And comes to his election presently.

Flourish of cornets.   Enter the PRINCE OF ARRAGON, PORTIA,
and their trains

PORTIA.   Behold, there stand the caskets, noble prince :
If you choose that wherein I am contain'd,   5
Straight shall our nuptial rites be solemnized :

SCENE IX Capell | Scene X   *Flourish* . . . omitted in Qq
Pope | Scene VIII Dyce.   6. rites Pope | rights QqFf.

   52. Enliven the sadness which he clings to or cherishes.

But if you fail, without more speech, my lord,
You must be gone from hence immediately.

ARRAGON. I am enjoin'd by oath to observe three things :
First, never to unfold to any one   10
Which casket 't was I chose ; next, if I fail
Of the right casket, never in my life
To woo a maid in way of marriage ;
Lastly, if I do fail in fortune of my choice,
Immediately to leave you and be gone.   15

PORTIA. To these injunctions every one doth swear
That comes to hazard for my worthless self.

ARRAGON. And so have I address'd me. Fortune now
To my heart's hope ! — Gold, silver, and base lead.
'Who chooseth me must give and hazard all he hath.'   20
You shall look fairer, ere I give or hazard.
What says the golden chest? ha ! let me see :
'Who chooseth me shall gain what many men desire.'
What many men desire ! That 'many' may be meant
By the fool multitude, that choose by show,   25
Not learning more than the fond eye doth teach ;
Which pries not to the interior, but, like the martlet,
Builds in the weather on the outward wall,
Even in the force and road of casualty.

7. you Qq | thou Ff.   27. pries F₁F₂ | payes F₃ | pays F₄.

13. **marriage.** A trisyllable. See Abbott, § 479.
14. **Lastly.** An interjectional line in the Cambridge Shakespeare.
Capell added it to the preceding line, making 'marriage' there a
dissyllable — a reading followed in previous editions of Hudson's
Shakespeare. The present text follows the Quartos and Folios.
18. **address'd :** prepared. Cf. use of 'address' as a golf term.
25. **By :** for. See Abbott, § 145.
29. Where it is exposed to every accident or mischance.

I will not choose what many men desire,   30
Because I will not jump with common spirits,
And rank me with the barbarous multitudes.
Why, then to thee, thou silver treasure-house ;
Tell me once more what title thou dost bear :
' Who chooseth me shall get as much as he deserves.'   35
And well said too ; for who shall go about
To cozen fortune, and be honourable
Without the stamp of merit?   Let none presume
To wear an undeserved dignity.
O, that estates, degrees, and offices   40
Were not deriv'd corruptly ! and that clear honour
Were purchas'd by the merit of the wearer !
How many then should cover that stand bare !
How many be commanded that command !
How much low peasantry would then be glean'd   45
From the true seed of honour ! and how much honour
Pick'd from the chaff and ruin of the times,
To be new-varnish'd ! Well, but to my choice :
' Who chooseth me shall get as much as he deserves.'
I will assume desert. — Give me a key for this,   50
And instantly unlock my fortunes here.

                         [*He opens the silver casket*]

45. **peasantry** Q2Q3Q4 | pezantry Q1 | pleasantry Ff.

31. **jump with** : agree with. So in *1 Henry IV*, I, ii, 78. In *The
Taming of the Shrew*, I, i, 195, we have the verb used absolutely ;
also in *Twelfth Night*, V, i, 259 : "till each circumstance Of place,
time, fortune, do cohere and jump That I am Viola."

43. How many then would keep their hats on who now stand
bareheaded as before their masters as superiors.

48. **new-varnish'd.** To prevent what he deemed a mixed metaphor,
Warburton suggested ' vanned,' i.e. ' winnowed.'

PORTIA. Too long a pause for that which you find there.

ARRAGON. What's here? the portrait of a blinking idiot,
Presenting me a schedule ! I will read it.

How much unlike art thou to Portia !   55

How much unlike my hopes and my deservings !

' Who chooseth me shall have as much as he deserves.'

Did I deserve no more than a fool's head?

Is that my prize? are my deserts no better?

PORTIA. To offend, and judge, are distinct offices,   60
And of opposed natures.

ARRAGON.   What is here?

> [*Reads*] The fire seven times tried this:
> Seven times tried that judgment is,
> That did never choose amiss.
> Some there be that shadows kiss;   65
> Such have but a shadow's bliss:
> There be fools alive, I wis,
> Silver'd o'er; and so was this.
> Take what wife you will to bed,
> I will ever be your head: 70
> So be gone: you are sped.

---

52. [Aside] Capell.   71. **gone** QqF1 | gone sir F2F3F4.

61. Portia is something of a lawyer, and she here has in mind the
old legal axiom, that no man is a good judge in his own case.

67. **I wis** : assuredly. The Middle English adverb *iwis*, or *ywis*
(German *gewiß*) came to be written *i wis* and, later, *I wis*, as if it
were subject and verb equivalent to the German *ich weiß*.

68. The idiot's portrait was inclosed in the silver casket, and in
that sense was 'silver'd o'er.'

69. An apparent oversight. The Prince was sworn "never to
woo a maid in way of marriage." But, of course, he might woo and
marry a widow !

70. You will always have a fool's head, whether married or not.

Still more fool I shall appear
By the time I linger here :
With one fool's head I came to woo,
But I go away with two.   75
Sweet, adieu. I 'll keep my oath,
Patiently to bear my wroth.

[*Exeunt* ARRAGON *and train*]

PORTIA. Thus hath the candle sing'd the moth.
O, these deliberate fools ! when they do choose,
They have the wisdom by their wit to lose.   80

NERISSA. The ancient saying is no heresy, —
Hanging and wiving goes by destiny.

PORTIA. Come, draw the curtain, Nerissa.

Enter a Servant

SERVANT. Where is my lady ?

PORTIA.   Here : what would my lord ?

SERVANT. Madam, there is alighted at your gate   85
A young Venetian, one that comes before
To signify the approaching of his lord,
From whom he bringeth sensible regreets ;
To wit, besides commends and courteous breath,

---

80. lose F₄ | loose F₁F₂F₃.   89. courteous Q₁Ff | curious Q₃Q₄.

84. **what would my lord.** A sportive reply to the servant's
"Where is my lady ? " So in *1 Henry IV*, II, iv, 314, the hostess
says to Prince Henry, " O Jesu ! my lord the prince ! " and he
replies, " How now, my lady the hostess ! "

88. **sensible regreets** : tangible greetings, greetings that may be
felt (for example, valuable presents). Or may the expression mean
' feeling salutations ' ? See *King John*, III, i, 241.

89. **commends** : compliments. See *Richard II*, III, i, 38. — **breath** :
words.

Gifts of rich value.   Yet I have not seen   90
So likely an ambassador of love :
A day in April never came so sweet,
To show how costly summer was at hand,
As this fore-spurrer comes before his lord.

PORTIA. No more, I pray thee : I am half afeard   95
Thou wilt say anon he is some kin to thee,
Thou spend'st such high-day wit in praising him. —
Come, come, Nerissa ; for I long to see
Quick Cupid's post that comes so mannerly.

NERISSA.   Bassanio, lord Love, if thy will it be !   100
                                            [*Exeunt*]

100. **Bassanio, lord Love,** Rowe | Bassanio Lord, love Q1Q2F1F2F3.

97. **high-day** : holiday, choice, finely phrased. Hotspur speaks of
"holiday and lady terms," *1 Henry IV*, I, iii, 46. Cf. the common
American expression, "Fourth-of-July eloquence."

ACT III

Scene I. *Venice. A street*

Enter SALANIO *and* SALARINO

SALANIO. Now, what news on the Rialto?

SALARINO. Why, yet it lives there uncheck'd, that Antonio hath a ship of rich lading wreck'd on the narrow seas; the Goodwins, I think they call the place; a very dangerous flat and fatal, where the carcasses of many a tall ship lie buried, as they say, if my gossip Report be an honest woman of her word.   7

SALANIO. I would she were as lying a gossip in that as ever knapp'd ginger, or made her neighbours believe she wept for the death of a third husband. But it is true, without any slips of prolixity, or crossing the plain highway of talk, that the good Antonio, the honest Antonio, — O, that I had a title good enough to keep his name company! —   13

3. wreck'd | wrackt F_1.

6. gossip Report $Q_2Q_3Q_4$ | gossips report Q_1Ff.

8. lying a F_1 | a lying Q_1.

12. honest Antonio | honest Antho. F_2.

3–4. narrow seas. A common name for the English Channel in the sixteenth century. Cf. II, viii, 28.

4. The Goodwin Sands lay off the eastern coast of Kent. The name was supposed to have been derived from Earl Godwin, whose lands were said to have been swallowed up there in the year 1099. In *King John*, V, v, 13, it is said that the supplies expected by the French "are cast away and sunk on Goodwin Sands."

9. knapp'd: gnawed, nibbled. Cotgrave translates *ronger* by 'knap.'

9–10. The presumption being that by that time she has got so used to the thing as not to mind it much.

SALARINO. Come, the full stop.

SALANIO. Ha ! what sayest thou? Why, the end is, he
hath lost a ship.   16

SALARINO. I would it might prove the end of his losses.

SALANIO. Let me say ' amen ' betimes, lest the devil cross
my prayer, for here he comes in the likeness of a Jew.

Enter SHYLOCK

How now, Shylock ! what news among the merchants?   20

SHYLOCK. You knew, none so well, none so well as you,
of my daughter's flight.

SALARINO. That 's certain : I, for my part, knew the tailor
that made the wings she flew withal.   24

SALANIO. And Shylock, for his own part, knew the bird
was fledg'd ; and then it is the complexion of them all to
leave the dam.   27

SHYLOCK. She is damn'd for it.

SALARINO. That 's certain, if the devil may be her judge.

SHYLOCK. My own flesh and blood to rebel !   30

SALANIO. Out upon it, old carrion ! rebels it at these years?

SHYLOCK. I say my daughter is my flesh and blood.   32

SALARINO. There is more difference between thy flesh and
hers than between jet and ivory ; more between your bloods
than there is between red wine and Rhenish. But tell us, do
you hear whether Antonio have had any loss at sea or no?

21. knew Q₂Ff | know Q₁.   32. and Q₁Ff | and my Q₂Q₃Q₄.

14. Finish the sentence, or Say on till you come to a period.
23–24. A sly allusion, probably, to the dress in which Jessica eloped.
— withal. The emphatic form of 'with.' So in l. 46. See Abbott, § 196.
26. complexion : natural inclination. So in *Hamlet*, I, iv, 27.
35. red wine and Rhenish : red wine and white.

SHYLOCK. There I have another bad match : a bank-rupt, a prodigal, who dare scarce show his head on the Rialto ; a beggar, that was us'd to come so smug upon the mart. Let him look to his bond : he was wont to call me usurer ; let him look to his bond : he was wont to lend money for a Christian courtesy ; let him look to his bond.   43

SALARINO. Why, I am sure, if he forfeit, thou wilt not take his flesh : what 's that good for?   45

SHYLOCK. To bait fish withal : if it will feed nothing else, it will feed my revenge. He hath disgrac'd me, and hin-der'd me half a million ; laugh'd at my losses, mock'd at my gains, scorn'd my nation, thwarted my bargains, cool'd my friends, heated mine enemies ; and what 's his reason? I am a Jew. Hath not a Jew eyes? hath not a Jew hands, organs, dimensions, senses, affections, passions? fed with the same food, hurt with the same weapons, subject to the same diseases, heal'd by the same means, warm'd and cool'd by the same winter and summer, as a Christian is? If you prick us, do we not bleed? if you tickle us, do we not laugh? if you poison us, do we not die? and if you wrong us, shall we not revenge? if we are like you in the rest, we will resemble you in that. If a Jew wrong a Christian, what is his humility? Revenge. If a Christian wrong a Jew, what should his sufferance be by Christian example? Why,

37-38. **bankrupt** Rowe | bankrout QqFf.

50. **his reason** Qq | the reason Ff.

52. **dimensions** Q_1 | dementions F_1.

39. **smug** : brisk, gay, spruce. Always, when applied to persons, 'smug' conveys the idea of self-satisfaction. In *1 Henry IV*, III, i, 102, Shakespeare speaks of "the smug and silver Trent."

47-48. Hindered me to the extent of half a million ducats.

60. **humility** : humanity. So in *Love's Labour 's Lost*, IV, iii, 349.

revenge. The villainy you teach me, I will execute; and
it shall go hard but I will better the instruction.   63

Enter a Servant

SERVANT. Gentlemen, my master Antonio is at his house,
and desires to speak with you both.   65

SALARINO. We have been up and down to seek him.

SALANIO. Here comes another of the tribe : a third cannot be match'd, unless the devil himself turn Jew.

[*Exeunt* SALANIO, SALARINO, *and* Servant]

Enter TUBAL

SHYLOCK. How now, Tubal! what news from Genoa?
hast thou found my daughter?   70

TUBAL. I often came where I did hear of her, but
cannot find her.   72

SHYLOCK. Why, there, there, there, there! a diamond
gone, cost me two thousand ducats in Frankfort! The
curse never fell upon our nation till now; I never felt it
till now : two thousand ducats in that; and other precious,
precious jewels. I would my daughter were dead at my
foot, and the jewels in her ear! would she were hears'd
at my foot, and the ducats in her coffin! No news of
them? — Why, so : — and I know not what's spent in the
search : why, thou loss upon loss! the thief gone with so
much, and so much to find the thief; and no satisfaction,
no revenge : nor no ill luck stirring but what lights on

64. Servant Rowe | man from
Anthonio F1.
80. what 's Qq | how much is Ff.

81. thou QqF1 | then F2F3F4.
83. lights on Q1 | lights a Q2Ff.

63. I shall not fail to surpass my teachers in this matter of revenge.

my shoulders ; no sighs but of my breathing ; no tears but
of my shedding.   85

TUBAL. Yes, other men have ill luck too : Antonio, as I
heard in Genoa, —

SHYLOCK. What, what, what? ill luck, ill luck?   88

TUBAL. Hath an argosy cast away, coming from Tripolis.

SHYLOCK. I thank God, I thank God !—Is it true, is it true ?

TUBAL. I spoke with some of the sailors that escap'd
the wreck.   92

SHYLOCK. I thank thee, good Tubal : good news, good
news ! ha, ha !— here in Genoa.

TUBAL. Your daughter spent in Genoa, as I heard, in
one night fourscore ducats.   96

SHYLOCK. Thou stick'st a dagger in me : I shall never see
my gold again : fourscore ducats at a sitting ! fourscore ducats !

TUBAL. There came divers of Antonio's creditors in my
company to Venice, that swear he cannot choose but break.

SHYLOCK. I am very glad of it : I 'll plague him ; I 'll
torture him : I am glad of it.   102

TUBAL. One of them show'd me a ring that he had of
your daughter for a monkey.   104

SHYLOCK. Out upon her ! Thou torturest me, Tubal : it
was my turquoise ; I had it of Leah when I was a bachelor :
I would not have given it for a wilderness of monkeys.

84-85. but of Q1 | but a Q2Ff.   95-96. in one Q1 | one Q2Ff.
90. is it . . . is it Q2Ff | ist . . . ist Q1.   106. turquoise Rowe | Turkies Q1
94. here QqFf | where ? Rowe.   Q2F1.

94. For a defense of the Quarto and Folio reading, see Furness.
106. The turquoise was held precious for its rarity and beauty and
for certain magical properties. It was supposed to have the power
of reconciling man and wife, and of forewarning the wearer of danger.
It was also thought to grow pale and dim if the wearer were ill.

TUBAL.   But Antonio is certainly undone.   108

SHYLOCK.   Nay, that's true, that's very true.   Go, Tubal,
fee me an officer; bespeak him a fortnight before.   I will
have the heart of him, if he forfeit; for, were he out of
Venice, I can make what merchandise I will.   Go, Tubal,
and meet me at our synagogue; go, good Tubal; at our
synagogue, Tubal.   [*Exeunt*]

SCENE II.   *Belmont.   A room in* PORTIA'S *house*

Enter BASSANIO, PORTIA, GRATIANO, NERISSA, *and* Attendants

PORTIA.   I pray you, tarry; pause a day or two
Before you hazard; for, in choosing wrong,
I lose your company : therefore forbear awhile.
There's something tells me — but it is not love —
I would not lose you; and you know yourself,   5
Hate counsels not in such a quality.
But, lest you should not understand me well, —
And yet a maiden hath no tongue but thought, —
I would detain you here some month or two
Before you venture for me.   I could teach you   10
How to choose right, but then I am forsworn;
So will I never be : so may you miss me;
But, if you do, you'll make me wish a sin,

112. **I will. Go** | I will: goe Q₂F₁
| I will go: go Q₁ | I will. Go, go
Johnson Camb.

3. **lose** | loose QqF₁.
5. **lose** Q₁F₂F₃F₄ | loose Q₂F₁.
11. **then I am** Q₂Ff | I am then Q₁.

109–110.   To fee an officer, or a lawyer, is to engage him by paying
for his services in advance.   Acceptance of such payment binds him.

112.   The editors of the Cambridge Shakespeare make Shylock
say here, "Go, go, Tubal," following what, in spite of the careless
punctuation, seems to be the reading of the First Quarto.

That I had been forsworn. Beshrew your eyes,
They have o'erlook'd me, and divided me ;   15
One half of me is yours, the other half yours. —
Mine own, I would say ; but if mine, then yours,
And so all yours ! O, these naughty times
Puts bars between the owners and their rights !
And so, though yours, not yours. Prove it so,   20
Let fortune go to hell for it, not I.
I speak too long ; but 't is to peize the time,
To eke it, and to draw it out in length,
To stay you from election.

BASSANIO.   Let me choose ;
For, as I am, I live upon the rack.   25

PORTIA. Upon the rack, Bassanio ! then confess
What treason there is mingled with your love.

BASSANIO. None but that ugly treason of mistrust,
Which makes me fear the enjoying of my love :
There may as well be amity and life   30
'Tween snow and fire, as treason and my love.

17. if Qq | of F₁ | first F₂F₃F₄.   23. eke Johnson | eck Q₁ | ich F₁.

19. **Puts.** So Quartos and First Folio. See Abbott, § 333.

20. **Prove it so**: should it prove so. If events should prove that I, who am yours in heart, am not to be yours in fact, let the punishment fall upon fortune for misdirecting your choice.

22. **peize**: retard. An old form of 'poise,' through Fr. *peiser* (*peser*) from Lat. *pensare*. The figure here involved is that of loading a thing in motion to make it go more slowly.

29. Shakespeare often has 'doubt' for 'fear' or 'suspect'; here he has 'fear' in the sense of 'doubt.' Fear the not enjoying of my love.

30. In previous editions of Hudson's Shakespeare, Walker's conjectural reading of 'league' for 'life' was adopted, as 'life' was considered a strange word for the place and made still more unfitting by what Bassanio says in his next speech.

PORTIA. Ay, but I fear you speak upon the rack,
Where men enforced do speak anything.

BASSANIO. Promise me life, and I'll confess the truth.

PORTIA. Well then, confess and live.

BASSANIO.   Confess and love
Had been the very sum of my confession :   36
O happy torment, when my torturer
Doth teach me answers for deliverance !
But let me to my fortune and the caskets.

PORTIA. Away, then ! I am lock'd in one of them :   40
If you do love me, you will find me out.
Nerissa, and the rest, stand all aloof.
Let music sound while he doth make his choice ;
Then, if he lose, he makes a swan-like end,
Fading in music : that the comparison   45
May stand more proper, my eye shall be the stream
And watery death-bed for him. He may win ;
And what is music then? Then music is
Even as the flourish when true subjects bow

33. do Qq | doth F1.

33. "It is pleasant to find Shakespeare before his age in denouncing
the futility of this barbarous method of extorting truth. He was old
enough to remember the case of Francis Throckmorton in 1584; and
that of Squires in 1598 was fresh in his mind." — Clar.

38. Doubtless many a poor man whose office it was to work the
rack, and whose heart had not been burnt to a cinder by theological
rancor, had pity on the victim, and whispered in his ear "answers
for deliverance," prompting him to speak what might suffice for
stopping the torture.

44-47. The allusion is to the popular belief that the swan sang
herself through the process of dying, 'fading (i.e. going out) in music.'
English poetry from Chaucer to Tennyson is full of exquisite references to this swan-lore. Cf. *Othello*, V, ii, 247; *King John*, V, vii, 21.

To a new-crowned monarch : such it is   50
As are those dulcet sounds in break of day
That creep into the dreaming bridegroom's ear,
And summon him to marriage. Now he goes,
With no less presence, but with much more love,
Than young Alcides, when he did redeem   55
The virgin tribute paid by howling Troy
To the sea-monster : I stand for sacrifice ;
The rest aloof are the Dardanian wives,
With bleared visages, come forth to view
The issue of the exploit. Go, Hercules !   60
Live thou, I live : with much much more dismay
I view the fight than thou that mak'st the fray.

Music, whilst BASSANIO *comments on the caskets to himself*

SONG

Tell me where is fancy bred,
Or in the heart or in the head?

61. **live: with** | live with QqF$_1$F$_2$. — **much much** Q$_2$F$_2$F$_3$ | much Q$_1$F$_1$.

50. At English coronations, the act of putting on the crown was signaled by a joyous flourish of trumpets ; whereupon the whole assembly were to bow their homage to the sovereign.

54. **presence** : dignity of mien, nobility of bearing, deportment.

57. The story, as told by Ovid, *Metamorphoses*, XI, is, that when Hesione, daughter of the Trojan king, was demanded by the sea-monster, and bound to a rock, Hercules slew the monster and delivered her. Bassanio goes "with much more love," because Hercules went, not from love of the lady, but to gain the reward of beautiful horses offered by Laomedon.

63. This song is very artfully conceived, and carries something enigmatical or riddle-like in its face, as if on purpose to suggest or hint darkly the way to the right choice. The clew, however, is such as to be seized only by a man whose heart is thoroughly right in the

How begot, how nourished?   65
    Reply, reply.
It is engender'd in the eyes,
With gazing fed; and fancy dies
In the cradle where it lies.
    Let us all ring fancy's knell;   70
    I 'll begin it, — Ding, dong, bell.
ALL.   Ding, dong, bell.

BASSANIO.   So may the outward shows be least themselves :
The world is still deceiv'd with ornament.
In law, what plea so tainted and corrupt,   75
But, being season'd with a gracious voice,
Obscures the show of evil?   In religion,

---

67. **eyes** Ff | eye Qq.   75. **tainted** QqF₂ | tanted F₁.

matter he goes about. 'Fancy,' as here used, means, apparently, that illusive power or action of the mind which has misled the other suitors, who, as Portia says, "have the wisdom by their wit to lose." And the illusion thus engendered in the eyes, and fed with gazing, dies just there where it is bred, as soon as it is brought to the test of experience by opening the wrong casket. The riddle evidently has some effect in starting Bassanio on the right track, by causing him to distrust such shows as catch the fancy or the eye, — the glitter of the gold and silver caskets.

66. **Reply, reply.** In Quartos and Folios these words stand in the margin, to the right of l. 65. This led to Hanmer's conjecture that 'Reply' was a stage direction, and Johnson and Steevens printed it as such — an arrangement adopted in previous editions of Hudson's Shakespeare. Capell prefixed '1 V.' (i.e. First Voice) to ll. 63, 64, 65, and '2 V.' to ll. 67, 68, 69, saying, "The words 'Reply, reply' show it to be a song in two parts or by two voices, followed by a chorus of divers assistant voices which 'all' indicates." The editors of the Cambridge Shakespeare say, "It is true that the words 'Reply, reply' stand in the margin of the old copies, but they are printed like the song in italics, and seem to be required as part of it by the rhythm and (if we read 'eye' with the Quartos) by the rhyme also."

What damned error, but some sober brow
Will bless it, and approve it with a text,
Hiding the grossness with fair ornament?   80
There is no vice so simple, but assumes
Some mark of virtue on his outward parts :
How many cowards, whose hearts are all as false
As stairs of sand, wear yet upon their chins
The beards of Hercules and frowning Mars ;   85
Who, inward search'd, have livers white as milk !
And these assume but valour's excrement
To render them redoubted ! Look on beauty,
And you shall see 'tis purchas'd by the weight ;
Which therein works a miracle in nature,   90

81. vice F2F3F4 | voice Q1F1 | 84. stairs F4 | staiers Q1 | stayers
voyce Q2Q3.   Q2F1Q3Q4 | stayres F2F3.

84. stairs. In previous editions of Hudson's Shakespeare, the
Folio reading 'stayers,' was adopted as a monosyllable in the sense
of 'props,' 'supports,' 'stays.'

86. Cowards were commonly spoken of as having white livers.
Shakespeare has 'lily-liver'd' and 'milk-liver'd' in the same sense ;
and Falstaff, 2 Henry IV, iv, iii, 110–114, instructs us that "The
second property of your excellent sherris is the warming of the
blood ; which, before cold and settled, left the liver white and pale,
which is the badge of pusillanimity and cowardice."

87. excrement. This word, from Lat. excresco, is used for everything which appears to grow or vegetate upon the human body, as
the hair, the beard, the nails. This is another illustration of the rule
that Shakespeare uses many words of Latin derivation in a sense
close to the original. See note, p. 7, l. 61.

89. The meaning here is not very obvious ; but the words are
probably to be construed in the light of what follows. It would
seem that false hair, "the golden tresses of the dead," was pur-
chased at so much an ounce ; and the more one had of it, the vainer
— the more frivolous or wanton — one was.

Making them lightest that wear most of it :
So are those crisped snaky golden locks,
Which makes such wanton gambols with the wind,
Upon supposed fairness, often known
To be the dowry of a second head,   95
The skull that bred them in the sepulchre.
Thus ornament is but the guiled shore
To a most dangerous sea ; the beauteous scarf
Veiling an Indian beauty ; in a word,

93. **makes** Ff | maketh Q₁Q₂.
97. **guiled** QqF₁ | guilded F₂F₃F₄
| gilded Rowe.

99. **an Indian beauty** QqF₂F₃ | an
Indian beautie F₁ | Indian; beauty's
Theobald's conjecture.

91. Another quibble upon ' light.' See note, p. 55, l. 42. Here, however, it is between ' light ' as opposed to ' heavy,' and ' light ' in the sense of ' frivolous ' or ' wanton.'

94. Upon supposed fairness : worn by fictitious beauty.

95. Shakespeare expresses a very strong dislike of the custom of wearing false hair, introduced into England early in Elizabeth's reign and very popular among the women of fashion. Cf. *Love's Labour's Lost*, IV, iii, 258 ; *Timon of Athens*, IV, iii, 144. In *Sonnets*, LXVIII, is a passage very like that in the text :

> Thus is his cheek the map of days outworn,
> When beauty lived and died as flowers do now,
>
> .   .   .   .
>
> Before the golden tresses of the dead,
> The right of sepulchres, were shorn away,
> To live a second life on second head ;
> Ere beauty's dead fleece made another gay.

96. The skull being in the sepulchre. Ablative absolute.

99. an Indian beauty. This is a famous Shakespeare *crux*. Upwards of twenty word-substitutes for ' beauty ' have been suggested. See Furness. In previous editions of Hudson's Shakespeare ' feature ' was the reading adopted. But, as it stands, the reading of Quartos and Folios is perfectly intelligible, ' an Indian beauty ' being simply one that standards of civilization and refinement would regard as no beauty at all.

The seeming truth which cunning times put on   100
To entrap the wisest. Therefore, thou gaudy gold,
Hard food for Midas, I will none of thee ;
Nor none of thee, thou pale and common drudge
'Tween man and man : but thou, thou meagre lead,
Which rather threatenest than dost promise aught,   105
Thy paleness moves me more than eloquence ;
And here choose I : joy be the consequence !

PORTIA. [*Aside*] How all the other passions fleet to air,
As doubtful thoughts, and rash-embrac'd despair,
And shuddering fear, and green-eyed jealousy !   110
O love, be moderate ; allay thy ecstasy ;
In measure rain thy joy ; scant this excess !
I feel too much thy blessing : make it less,
For fear I surfeit !

BASSANIO.   What find I here?

                              [*Opening the leaden casket*]

Fair Portia's counterfeit ! What demi-god   115
Hath come so near creation? Move these eyes?

---

101. **Therefore** Q1F2F3 | therefore   106. **paleness** QqFf | plainness
then Q2F1.   Warburton Theobald.
102. **food** Q2Ff | foole Q1.   112. **rain** F3F4 | reine Q3Q4 |
105. **aught** Theobald | ought QqFf.   range Q1 | raine Q2F1F2.

102. **Midas**, king of Phrygia, asked of Dionysus (Bacchus) that
whatever he touched might be turned into gold. The request being
granted, and all his food turning to gold as it touched his lips, he
implored Dionysus to revoke the favor. See Ovid, *Metamorphoses*, XI.

106. **paleness**. This — the reading of Quartos and Folios — Warburton changed to 'plainness,' which Staunton adopted with the
remark that the 'plainness' which moves Bassanio 'more than eloquence' is the plain speaking of the inscription on the leaden coffer,
contrasted with the tempting labels of its neighbors.

115. **counterfeit**: portrait. Cf. *Timon of Athens*, V, i, 83.

Or whether, riding on the balls of mine,
Seem they in motion? Here are sever'd lips,
Parted with sugar breath : so sweet a bar
Should sunder such sweet friends. Here in her hairs   120
The painter plays the spider, and hath woven
A golden mesh to entrap the hearts of men,
Faster than gnats in cobwebs. But her eyes ! —
How could he see to do them? having made one,
Methinks it should have power to steal both his   125
And leave itself unfurnish'd. Yet look, how far
The substance of my praise doth wrong this shadow
In underprizing it, so far this shadow
Doth limp behind the substance. Here 's the scroll,
The continent and summary of my fortune :   130

　　[*Reads*] You that choose not by the view,
　　　　　Chance as fair, and choose as true !
　　　　　Since this fortune falls to you,
　　　　　Be content, and seek no new.
　　　　　If you be well pleas'd with this,   135
　　　　　And hold your fortune for your bliss,
　　　　　Turn you where your lady is,
　　　　　And claim her with a loving kiss.

A gentle scroll. — Fair lady, by your leave ;
I come by note, to give and to receive.   140

---

117. **whether** Ff | whither Q1Q2.　　　126. **unfurnish'd** QqFf | unfinish'd
122. **to entrap** | t' intrap Q1Ff.　　Rowe.

126. **unfurnish'd**: unmated. In *Hamlet*, V, ii, 150, occurs 'unfellowed.'
130. **continent**: that which contains. The literal meaning of the Latin.
139. Here Rowe introduced stage direction ' Kissing her.'
140. I come in accordance with the written direction to give a
kiss and to receive the lady. — **note.** Cf. *The Winter's Tale*, IV, iii, 49.

Like one of two contending in a prize,
That thinks he hath done well in people's eyes,
Hearing applause and universal shout,
Giddy in spirit, still gazing, in a doubt
Whether those peals of praise be his or no;   145
So, thrice-fair lady, stand I, even so;
As doubtful whether what I see be true,
Until confirm'd, sign'd, ratified by you.

PORTIA. You see me, Lord Bassanio, where I stand,
Such as I am: though for myself alone   150
I would not be ambitious in my wish,
To wish myself much better; yet for you
I would be trebled twenty times myself;
A thousand times more fair, ten thousand times more rich;
That, only to stand high in your account,   155
I might in virtues, beauties, livings, friends,
Exceed account: but the full sum of me
Is sum of — something; which, to term in gross,
Is an unlesson'd girl, unschool'd, unpractis'd:
Happy in this, she is not yet so old   160
But she may learn; happier than this,
She is not bred so dull but she can learn;

145. peals Q₂Ff | pearles Q₁.
149. see me, Lord Qq | see my Lord F₁F₂F₃ | see, my Lord F₄.
154. more rich | Camb prints as separate line | in QqFf part of l. 155.

158. something Qq | nothing Ff.
161. happier than this Camb | happier then this QqF₁ | happier then in this F₂F₃F₄ | more happy then in this Pope.

158. The dash before 'something' indicates that Portia hesitates for a term with which to describe herself modestly, yet without any affectation of modesty. The Folio reading 'nothing' savors too much of affectation of humility to accord well with Portia's character. Besides, she seems to be playing with the likeness of sound in 'sum' and 'some.' — term in gross: define generally.

Happiest of all is that her gentle spirit
Commits itself to yours to be directed,
As from her lord, her governor, her king.   165
Myself and what is mine to you and yours
Is now converted : but now I was the lord
Of this fair mansion, master of my servants,
Queen o'er myself ; and even now, but now,
This house, these servants, and this same myself,   170
Are yours, my lord : I give them with this ring ;
Which when you part from, lose, or give away,
Let it presage the ruin of your love,
And be my vantage to exclaim on you.

BASSANIO. Madam, you have bereft me of all words ;   175
Only my blood speaks to you in my veins ;
And there is such confusion in my powers,
As, after some oration fairly spoke
By a beloved prince, there doth appear
Among the buzzing pleased multitude ;   180
Where every something, being blent together,
Turns to a wild of nothing, save of joy,
Express'd and not express'd.   But when this ring
Parts from this finger, then parts life from hence :
O, then be bold to say Bassanio 's dead !   185

NERISSA. My lord and lady, it is now our time,
That have stood by and seen our wishes prosper,
To cry, good joy.   Good joy, my Lord and lady !

GRATIANO. My Lord Bassanio and my gentle lady,
I wish you all the joy that you can wish ;   190

167. The 'lord' of a thing is, properly, the owner of it ; hence the
word is applicable to a woman as well as to a man.

174. vantage: opportunity. — exclaim on: reproach loudly.

For I am sure you can wish none from me.

And, when your honours mean to solemnize

The bargain of your faith, I do beseech you,

Even at that time I may be married too.   194

    BASSANIO. With all my heart, so thou canst get a wife.

    GRATIANO. I thank your lordship, you have got me one.

My eyes, my lord, can look as swift as yours :

You saw the mistress, I beheld the maid ;

You lov'd, I lov'd ; for intermission

No more pertains to me, my lord, than you.   200

Your fortune stood upon the caskets there,

And so did mine too, as the matter falls ;

For, wooing here, until I sweat again,

And swearing, till my very roof was dry

With oaths of love, at last, if promise last,   205

I got a promise of this fair one here

---

196. **have** QqF₂F₃F₄ | gave F₁.

199. **lov'd** ; **for intermission No more** Theobald | lov'd for intermission, No more Q₁Q₂F₁F₂F₃ | loved for intermission. No more Camb.

201. **caskets** Q₂Ff | casket Q₁Q₃ Q₄.

203. **here** Pope | heere QqF₁ | heete F₂ | heat F₃F₄ | herd Rowe (1 ed.) | her Rowe (2 ed.).

191. You have so much joy in each other, that you cannot grudge any to me. This is Johnson's interpretation. Abbott suggests : " none which I do not wish you," § 158.

198. We are not to understand by this that Nerissa is merely a servant-maid to Portia : she holds the place of companion or friend, and Portia all along treats her as such. They are as nearly equals in rank as Bassanio and Gratiano are, who are a pair of friends, not master and servant. Nor does it conflict with this, that Gratiano speaks of Portia as "her mistress" ; for he is in a position that requires him to plead his present cause with a good deal of modesty and deference, lest he should seem to have abused his privilege of accompanying Bassanio on this loving voyage.

199. **intermission** : delay. Gratiano means, apparently, that, following his example, he had been as prompt to fall in love as Bassanio.

To have her love, provided that your fortune
Achiev'd her mistress.

PORTIA.   Is this true, Nerissa?

NERISSA. Madam, it is, so you stand pleas'd withal.

BASSANIO. And do you, Gratiano, mean good faith? 210

GRATIANO. Yes, faith, my lord.

BASSANIO. Our feast shall be much honour'd in your
    marriage.

GRATIANO. But who comes here? Lorenzo and his infidel?
What, and my old Venetian friend, Salerio?

Enter LORENZO, JESSICA, *and* SALERIO

BASSANIO. Lorenzo and Salerio, welcome hither;   215
If that the youth of my new interest here

205. it is, so you Qq | it is so, so you Ff.   214. Scene III Pope.

214. **Salerio.** Is this a new character, or is the name simply a mis-
spelling for Salarino or Salanio? Rowe held that the Salerio of the
Quartos and Folios was a misprint for Salanio, and he substituted
the one name for the other wherever it occurred. Capell restored
Salerio in the text, though he believed it to be an abbreviation of
Salerino, or, as it is printed in the present text, Salarino. Steevens
was the first to add Salerio to the list of Dramatis Personæ as a
character distinct from Salanio and Salarino. A good case can be
made out for this Salerio being but the Salanio who appears in the
first scene of the play as the common friend of Antonio, Bassanio, and
Salarino. It is easy to see how the mistake might arise, for the similar
names, Salanio and Salarino, are spelled in Quartos and Folios in
nine different ways, and the various abbreviations of the names add
to the confusion and complication. On the other hand, in both Quartos and Folios the name Salerio is spelled in full every time it occurs;
and is not the whimsicality in introducing here a third character
whose name begins with 'Sal-' thoroughly Shakespearian and in
keeping with the dramatist's delight in word quibble and equivoque?
There are two Jaqueses in the Dramatis Personæ of *As You Like It*.

Have power to bid you welcome. — By your leave,
I bid my very friends and countrymen,
Sweet Portia, welcome.

PORTIA.   So do I, my lord ;
They are entirely welcome.   220

LORENZO. I thank your honour. — For my part, my lord,
My purpose was not to have seen you here ;
But, meeting with Salerio by the way,
He did entreat me, past all saying nay,
To come with him along.

SALERIO.   I did, my lord ;   225
And I have reason for it. Signior Antonio
Commends him to you.   [*Gives* BASSANIO *a letter*]

BASSANIO.   Ere I ope his letter,
I pray you, tell me how my good friend doth.

SALERIO. Not sick, my lord, unless it be in mind ;
Nor well, unless in mind : his letter there   230
Will show you his estate.

GRATIANO. Nerissa, cheer yon stranger; bid her welcome.—
Your hand, Salerio : what's the news from Venice?
How doth that royal merchant, good Antonio?
I know he will be glad of our success ;   235
We are the Jasons, we have won the fleece.

SALERIO. I would you had won the fleece that he hath lost !

PORTIA. There are some shrewd contents in yon same
          paper,
That steals the colour from Bassanio's cheek :
Some dear friend dead ; else nothing in the world   240

234. **royal merchant.** See note, p. 102, l. 29.
236. Cf. Marlowe, *The Jew of Malta*, IV, iv, 99.
238. **shrewd**: evil. Properly p. part. of *shrewen*, 'to curse.'

Could turn so much the constitution
Of any constant man. What, worse and worse ! —
With leave, Bassanio ; I am half yourself,
And I must freely have the half of anything
That this same paper brings you.

BASSANIO.   O sweet Portia,   245
Here are a few of the unpleasant'st words
That ever blotted paper ! Gentle lady,
When I did first impart my love to you,
I freely told you, all the wealth I had
Ran in my veins, — I was a gentleman ;   250
And then I told you true : and yet, dear lady,
Rating myself at nothing, you shall see
How much I was a braggart. When I told you
My state was nothing, I should then have told you
That I was worse than nothing ; for, indeed,   255
I have engag'd myself to a dear friend,
Engag'd my friend to his mere enemy,
To feed my means. Here is a letter, lady ;
The paper as the body of my friend,
And every word in it a gaping wound,   260
Issuing life-blood. — But is it true, Salerio?
Hath all his ventures fail'd ? What, not one hit?
From Tripolis, from Mexico, and England,
From Lisbon, Barbary, and India?

---

253. braggart QqF₁F₂F₃ | beggar F₄.   262. Hath QqFf | have Pope.

244. Pope omitted 'freely' in this line, regarding it as redundancy.
As the word 'freely' occurs five lines after, it was thought to have
crept in here out of place by a compositor's slip.

246. unpleasant'st. "*Est* in superlatives is often pronounced *st*
after dentals and liquids." See Abbott, § 473.

And not one vessel scape the dreadful touch   265
Of merchant-marring rocks?

    SALERIO.   Not one, my lord.
Besides, it should appear that, if he had
The present money to discharge the Jew,
He would not take it. Never did I know
A creature, that did bear the shape of man,   270
So keen and greedy to confound a man:
He plies the Duke at morning and at night;
And doth impeach the freedom of the state,
If they deny him justice: twenty merchants,
The Duke himself, and the magnificoes   275
Of greatest port, have all persuaded with him;
But none can drive him from the envious plea
Of forfeiture, of justice, and his bond.

    JESSICA. When I was with him, I have heard him swear,
To Tubal and to Chus, his countrymen,   280
That he would rather have Antonio's flesh
Than twenty times the value of the sum
That he did owe him: and I know, my lord,
If law, authority, and power deny not,
It will go hard with poor Antonio.   285

    PORTIA. Is it your dear friend that is thus in trouble?

    BASSANIO. The dearest friend to me, the kindest man,
The best-condition'd and unwearied spirit
In doing courtesies; and one in whom

---

   273. impeach the freedom: call in question the reputation of the
state for granting equal rights to every one. Cf. IV, i, 39.

   288. unwearied. For ellipsis of superlative inflection, see Abbott,
§ 398. See note, p. 35, l. 46. So we have in *Sonnets*, LXXX, 6:

       The humble as the proudest sail doth bear.

The ancient Roman honour more appears 290
Than any that draws breath in Italy.
    PORTIA. What sum owes he the Jew?
    BASSANIO. For me three thousand ducats.
    PORTIA.   What, no more?
Pay him six thousand, and deface the bond;
Double six thousand, and then treble that, 295
Before a friend of this description
Shall lose a hair through Bassanio's fault.
First go with me to church and call me wife,
And then away to Venice to your friend;
For never shall you lie by Portia's side 300
With an unquiet soul. You shall have gold
To pay the petty debt twenty times over:
When it is paid, bring your true friend along.
My maid Nerissa and myself meantime
Will live as maids and widows. Come, away! 305
For you shall hence upon your wedding-day:
Bid your friends welcome, show a merry cheer:
Since you are dear bought, I will love you dear.
But let me hear the letter of your friend. 309
    BASSANIO. [*Reads*]

Sweet Bassanio, my ships have all miscarried, my creditors
grow cruel, my estate is very low, my bond to the Jew is forfeit; and since in paying it, it is impossible I should live, all
debts are cleared between you and I, if I might but see you

---

293. **What, no more** Ff | in Qq part   297. **through** QqF1 | through my
of l. 294.   F2F3F4.
    296. **this** QqFf | his S. Walker conj.   313. **but see** Qq | see Ff.

307. **cheer**: countenance. Middle English *chere* from Low Lat. *cara*.
313. **between you and I**. In Jespersen's *Progress in Language* this
usage, common in Elizabethan literature, is explained thus: "*I* was

at my death.   Notwithstanding, use your pleasure; if your love
do not persuade you to come, let not my letter.   315

PORTIA.   O love, dispatch all business, and be gone !
BASSANIO.   Since I have your good leave to go away,
  I will make haste; but, till I come again,
No bed shall e'er be guilty of my stay,   319
    Nor rest be interposer 'twixt us twain.   [*Exeunt*]

SCENE III. *Venice. A street*

Enter SHYLOCK, SALARINO, ANTONIO, *and* Jailer

SHYLOCK.   Jailer, look to him : tell not me of mercy. —
This is the fool that lends out money gratis. —
Jailer, look to him.
ANTONIO.   Hear me yet, good Shylock.
SHYLOCK.   I'll have my bond; speak not against my bond :
I have sworn an oath that I will have my bond.   5
Thou call'dst me dog before thou hadst a cause ;
But, since I am a dog, beware my fangs :
The Duke shall grant me justice. — I do wonder,
Thou naughty jailer, that thou art so fond
To come abroad with him at his request.   10
ANTONIO.   I pray thee, hear me speak.

320. **Nor** Q2Ff | No Q1.   SALARINO Q1 | Solanio F1 | Salerio Q2.
SCENE III | Scene IV Pope.   2. **lends** Ff | lent Qq.

preferred to *me* after *and*, because the group of words *you and I*,
he and I, etc., in which this particular word-order was required by
common politeness, would occur in every-day speech so frequently
as to make it practically a kind of stock-phrase taken as a whole,
the last word of which was therefore not inflected."

9. **naughty**: wicked. Cf. *King Lear*, III, vii, 37. — **fond**: foolish.

SHYLOCK. I 'll have my bond ; I will not hear thee speak :
I 'll have my bond ; and therefore speak no more.
I 'll not be made a soft and dull-eyed fool,
To shake the head, relent, and sigh, and yield   15
To Christian intercessors.   Follow not ;
I 'll have no speaking : I will have my bond.   [*Exit*]

SALARINO. It is the most impenetrable cur
That ever kept with men.

ANTONIO.   Let him alone :
I 'll follow him no more with bootless prayers.   20
He seeks my life ; his reason well I know :
I oft deliver'd from his forfeitures
Many that have at times made moan to me ;
Therefore he hates me.

SALARINO.   I am sure the Duke
Will never grant this forfeiture to hold.   25

ANTONIO. The Duke cannot deny the course of law :
For the commodity that strangers have
With us in Venice, if it be denied,
Will much impeach the justice of the state ;

24-25. Printed as prose in $F_2F_3F_4$.   29. the state Q_2Ff | his state Q_1.

19. kept: dwelt. So in *Measure for Measure*, III, i, 10.
27. commodity : commercial privileges.
26-29. In previous editions of Hudson's Shakespeare, the Capell
reading and punctuation were adopted here :

> The Duke cannot deny the course of law,
> For the commodity that strangers have
> With us in Venice : if it be denied,
> 'T will much impeach the justice of the State. . . .

Here 'for' would mean 'because of.'
Antonio was one of the citizens, while Shylock was reckoned
among the strangers of the place. And, since the city was benefited

Since that the trade and profit of the city   30
Consisteth of all nations. Therefore, go :
These griefs and losses have so bated me,
That I shall hardly spare a pound of flesh
To-morrow to my bloody creditor.—
Well, jailer, on. — Pray God, Bassanio come   35
To see me pay his debt, and then I care not !   [*Exeunt*]

SCENE IV. *Belmont. A room in* PORTIA'S *house*

Enter PORTIA, NERISSA, LORENZO, JESSICA, *and* BALTHASAR

LORENZO. Madam, although I speak it in your presence,
You have a noble and a true conceit
Of god-like amity ; which appears most strongly
In bearing thus the absence of your lord.
But, if you knew to whom you show this honour,   5
How true a gentleman you send relief,
How dear a lover of my lord your husband,
I know you would be prouder of the work
Than customary bounty can enforce you.

PORTIA. I never did repent for doing good,   10
Nor shall not now : for in companions

SCENE IV Rowe | Scene V Pope. BALTHASAR | a man of Portia's QqFf.

as much by the trade of foreigners as of natives, justice required the
law to give equal advantages to both. But to stop the course of
law in behalf of citizens against strangers would clearly impeach the
justice of the state.

32. **bated** : lowered, reduced. Cf. IV, i, 71.

6. **gentleman**. The dative case. Modern English allows such a dative
(without 'to') only when it comes between the verb and its accusative.

7. **lover** : friend. So in *Coriolanus*, V, ii, 14.

That do converse and waste the time together,
Whose souls do bear an equal yoke of love,
There must be needs a like proportion
Of lineaments, of manners, and of spirit;   15
Which makes me think that this Antonio,
Being the bosom lover of my lord,
Must needs be like my lord. If it be so,
How little is the cost I have bestow'd
In purchasing the semblance of my soul   20
From out the state of hellish cruelty!
This comes too near the praising of myself;
Therefore no more of it: hear other things.
Lorenzo, I commit into your hands
The husbandry and manage of my house   25
Until my lord's return: for mine own part,
I have toward heaven breath'd a secret vow
To live in prayer and contemplation,
Only attended by Nerissa here,
Until her husband and my lord's return: 30
There is a monastery two miles off,
And there we will abide. I do desire you
Not to deny this imposition,
The which my love and some necessity
Now lays upon you.

    LORENZO.   Madam, with all my heart,   35
I shall obey you in all fair commands.

    PORTIA. My people do already know my mind,

---

13. equal Q₁ | egall Q₂ | egal F₁F₂.   heere other things QqF₁F₂ | here
21. cruelty Q₂Ff | misery Q₁.   other things, F₃F₄.
23. hear other things.   Theobald | 32. we will Q₂Ff | will we Q₁.

   25. husbandry: stewardship. — manage: management.

And will acknowledge you and Jessica
In place of Lord Bassanio and myself.
So fare you well, till we shall meet again.   40

   LORENZO.   Fair thoughts and happy hours attend on you !

   JESSICA.   I wish your ladyship all heart's content.

   PORTIA.   I thank you for your wish, and am well pleas'd
To wish it back on you : fare you well, Jessica. —

                   [*Exeunt* JESSICA *and* LORENZO]
Now, Balthasar,   45
As I have ever found thee honest-true,
So let me find thee still. Take this same letter,
And use thou all the endeavour of a man
In speed to Padua : see thou render this
Into my cousin's hand, Doctor Bellario ;   50
And, look, what notes and garments he doth give thee,
Bring them, I pray thee, with imagin'd speed
Unto the tranect, to the common ferry
Which trades to Venice. Waste no time in words,
But get thee gone : I shall be there before thee.   55

   BALTHASAR. Madam, I go with all convenient speed. [*Exit*]

   PORTIA. Come on, Nerissa ; I have work in hand
That you yet know not of : we 'll see our husbands
Before they think of us.

   NERISSA.   Shall they see us ?

---

40. **So fare you well** F2F3F4Q3Q4
| So far you well Q2F1 | And so fare-
well Q1.

45-46. Printed as one line in QqFf.
49. **Padua** Theobald | Mantua Qq
Ff.

52. **imagin'd speed** : with the celerity of imagination. So in the
Chorus before *Henry V*, Act III : " Thus with imagined wing our
swift scene flies." So Steevens interprets. Abbott, § 375, takes
' imagined ' as meaning ' imaginable.'

53. **tranect**. Most probably this much-discussed word is but a
misprint, for ' traject ' (crossing, ferry). Cf. Ital. *traghetto* (*tragetto*).

PORTIA. They shall, Nerissa; but in such a habit,   60
That they shall think we are accomplished
With that we lack. I 'll hold thee any wager,
When we are both accoutred like young men,
I 'll prove the prettier fellow of the two,
And wear my dagger with the braver grace;   65
And speak between the change of man and boy
With a reed voice; and turn two mincing steps
Into a manly stride; and speak of frays,
Like a fine-bragging youth; and tell quaint lies,
How honourable ladies sought my love,   70
Which I denying, they fell sick and died;
I could not do withal: then I 'll repent,
And wish, for all that, that I had not kill'd them.
And twenty of these puny lies I 'll tell;
That men shall swear I have discontinued school   75
Above a twelvemonth. I have within my mind
A thousand raw tricks of these bragging Jacks,
Which I will practise.
But come; I 'll tell thee all my whole device
When I am in my coach, which stays for us   80
At the park gate; and therefore haste away,
For we must measure twenty miles to-day.   [*Exeunt*]

62. that QqFf | what Rowe   63. accoutred | accoutered Q2Ff |
(2 ed.).   apparreld Q1.

72. I could not do withal: I could not help it. A phrase of the
time. "In Florio's *Giardino di Ricreatione* (1591) the Italian '*Io
non saprei farci altro*' is rendered into English 'I cannot doo with
all.'"— Camb. So in Fletcher and Massinger's (?) *The Little French
Lawyer:* "I cannot do withal; I have spoke and spoke; I am
betrayed and lost too."

77. Jacks: saucy fellows. An Elizabethan term of contempt.

SCENE V. *The same. A garden*

Enter LAUNCELOT *and* JESSICA

LAUNCELOT. Yes, truly; for, look you, the sins of the father are to be laid upon the children : therefore, I promise ye, I fear you. I was always plain with you, and so now I speak my agitation of the matter : therefore be of good cheer; for, truly, I think you are damn'd. There is but one hope in it that can do you any good; and that is but a kind of bastard hope neither.   7

JESSICA. And what hope is that, I pray thee?

LAUNCELOT. Marry, you may partly hope that you are not the Jew's daughter.

JESSICA. That were a kind of bastard hope, indeed : so the sins of my mother should be visited upon me.   12

LAUNCELOT. Truly then I fear you are damn'd both by father and mother : thus when I shun Scylla, your father, I fall into Charybdis, your mother : well, you are gone both ways.   16

SCENE V | Scene VI Pope.   3. ye Q1 | you Q2Ff.
LAUNCELOT Rowe | Clowne Ff.   4. be of Ff | be a Q1Q2.

3. **fear**: fear for. So in l. 28. Cf. *Richard III*, I, i, 137.

14–15. This refers to a proverbial saying which has been traced back as far as to St. Augustine : "*Ne iterum quasi fugiens Charybdim, in Scyllam incurras.*" Malone quotes in this connection a line in the *Alexandreis* of Philippe Gualtier (Gaultier), the thirteenth century poet : "*Incidis in Scyllam, cupiens vitare Charybdim.*" This became a common proverb, both in the original Latin and in English versions. For example, in Roger Ascham's *Scholemaster* we find : "If Scylla drown him not, Charybdis may fortune to swallow him." Halliwell quotes an old Somersetshire proverb to the same purpose : "He got out of the muxy and fell into the pucksy."

JESSICA. I shall be sav'd by my husband; he hath made
me a Christian.   18

LAUNCELOT. Truly, the more to blame he: we were
Christians enow before; e'en as many as could well live,
one by another. This making of Christians will raise the
price of hogs: if we grow all to be pork-eaters, we shall
not shortly have a rasher on the coals for money.   23

JESSICA. I 'll tell my husband, Launcelot, what you say:
here he comes.

Enter LORENZO

LORENZO. I shall grow jealous of you shortly, Launcelot,
if you thus get my wife into corners.   27

JESSICA. Nay, you need not fear us, Lorenzo: Launcelot
and I are out. He tells me flatly, there is no mercy for me
in heaven, because I am a Jew's daughter: and he says, you
are no good member of the commonwealth; for, in convert-
ing Jews to Christians, you raise the price of pork.   32

LORENZO. I think the best grace of wit will shortly turn
into silence, and discourse grow commendable in none only
but parrots. — Go in, sirrah; bid them prepare for dinner.

LAUNCELOT. That is done, sir; they have all stomachs.

LORENZO. Goodly Lord, what a wit-snapper are you!
then bid them prepare dinner.   38

LAUNCELOT. That is done too, sir; only, 'cover' is the
word.

LORENZO. Will you cover, then, sir?

LAUNCELOT. Not so, sir, neither; I know my duty.   42

---

20. enow. A dialect form, but often used as the plural of 'enough.'
39. Launcelot is playing upon the word 'cover,' which was used
both for setting the table and for putting on the hat.

LORENZO. Yet more quarrelling with occasion ! Wilt thou show the whole wealth of thy wit in an instant? I pray thee, understand a plain man in his plain meaning : go to thy fellows, bid them cover the table, serve in the meat, and we will come in to dinner.   47

LAUNCELOT. For the table, sir, it shall be serv'd in; for the meat, sir, it shall be cover'd ; for your coming in to dinner, sir, why, let it be as humours and conceits shall govern. [*Exit*]

LORENZO. O dear discretion, how his words are suited !
The fool hath planted in his memory   52
An army of good words ; and I do know
A many fools, that stand in better place,
Garnish'd like him, that for a tricksy word   55
Defy the matter. — How cheer'st thou, Jessica?
And now, good sweet, say thy opinion :
How dost thou like the Lord Bassanio's wife?

JESSICA. Past all expressing. It is very meet
The Lord Bassanio live an upright life ;   60
For, having such a blessing in his lady,
He finds the joys of heaven here on earth ;

56. cheer'st FfQ₃Q₄ | cherst Q₂ | far'st Q₁.

43. quarrelling with occasion. "At odds with the matter in question." — Schmidt. Launcelot's punning is irrelevant to the matter in hand.

56. Defy the matter: set the meaning at defiance. 'To defy' was often used for 'to renounce,' 'to forsake,' or 'to give up.' So in *I Henry IV*, I, iii, 228 :

> All studies here I solemnly defy,
> Save how to gall and pinch this Bolingbroke.

Shakespeare seems to have reference to the habit, which infected all classes in the last decade of the sixteenth century, of sacrificing matter, or letting it go, in fondness for verbal trickery and chase after puns and plays upon words. — cheer'st : farest.

And if on earth he do not mean it, then
In reason he should never come to heaven.
Why, if two gods should play some heavenly match,   65
And on the wager lay two earthly women,
And Portia one, there must be something else
Pawn'd with the other; for the poor rude world
Hath not her fellow.

LORENZO.   Even such a husband
Hast thou of me as she is for a wife.   70

JESSICA. Nay, but ask my opinion too of that.

LORENZO. I will anon : first, let us go to dinner.

JESSICA. Nay, let me praise you while I have a stomach.

LORENZO. No, pray thee, let it serve for table-talk;
Then, howsoe'er thou speak'st, 'mong other things   75
I shall digest it.

JESSICA.   Well, I 'll set you forth.   [*Exeunt*]

63-64. **mean it, then** In | meane | mean it, it Is Ff | meane it, In
it, then In Q1 | meane it, it In Q2   Q3Q4 | merit it, In Pope.

63–64. Another famous *crux*. In previous editions of Hudson's
Shakespeare Pope's emendation was adopted, 'it' being supposed
to have reference to 'blessing' in l. 61. The reading in the text is
that of the First Quarto. Many explanations and at least twelve
text emendations have been offered. Capell explained 'mean it' by
'observe moderation,' and Furness and Corson interpret it in the
same way. But is this not going too far afield ? Shakespeare never
uses 'mean' in this sense as a verb. Does not Jessica say simply
and poetically that Bassanio, having the joys of heaven here on earth
in his possession of Portia, ought to lead almost as upright a life as
he would were he in heaven ? If not, he ought never to get to heaven.
Then she goes on to tell of the heavenly qualities of Portia.

64. **come to heaven.** Cf. Lorenzo's words, II, iv, 33.

68. **pawn'd** : wagered. Cf. *Coriolanus*, III, i, 15.

73. An equivoque on 'stomach,' which means 'disposition' or
'inclination,' as well as appetite for food.

ACT IV

SCENE I. *Venice. A court of justice*

Enter the DUKE, *the* Magnificoes, ANTONIO, BASSANIO,
GRATIANO, SALERIO, *and others*

DUKE. What, is Antonio here?

ANTONIO. Ready, so please your Grace.

DUKE. I am sorry for thee : thou art come to answer
A stony adversary, an inhuman wretch
Uncapable of pity, void and empty   5
From any dram of mercy.

ANTONIO.   I have heard
Your Grace hath ta'en great pains to qualify
His rigorous course ; but, since he stands obdurate,
And that no lawful means can carry me
Out of his envy's reach, I do oppose   10
My patience to his fury ; and am arm'd
To suffer, with a quietness of spirit,
The very tyranny and rage of his.

DUKE. Go one, and call the Jew into the court.   14

SALERIO. He is ready at the door : he comes, my lord.

7-8. Printed as three lines in Q1.   **15.** SALERIO Q2Q3Q4 | Sal. Q1Ff.

1. What. An exclamation of attention, not surprise. Cf. "Hwaet!"
in the opening line of *Beowulf*. Cf. ll. 46, 110.

9. that: because. See Abbott, § 285.

10. envy's : malice's. So 'envious' in the sense of 'malicious' in
I-II, ii, 277. Cf. *Romeo and Juliet*, III, i, 173.

Enter SHYLOCK

DUKE. Make room, and let him stand before our face. —
Shylock, the world thinks, and I think so too,
That thou but lead'st this fashion of thy malice
To the last hour of act; and then 'tis thought
Thou 'lt show thy mercy and remorse, more strange   20
Than is thy strange apparent cruelty;
And where thou now exact'st the penalty,
Which is a pound of this poor merchant's flesh,
Thou wilt not only loose the forfeiture,
But, touch'd with human gentleness and love,   25
Forgive a moiety of the principal;
Glancing an eye of pity on his losses,
That have of late so huddled on his back,
Enow to press a royal merchant down,
And pluck commiseration of his state   30
From brassy bosoms and rough hearts of flint,

25. **human** Rowe | humane Q_1Ff.   31. **flint** Q_1 | flints Q_2F_1.

18–21. Keepest up this manner or appearance of malice to the
latest minute, and then thou wilt show pity.

20. **remorse**: pity. So in *Macbeth*, I, v, 45.

26. **moiety**. This word is used fifteen times by Shakespeare;
never in the etymological sense of 'a half' (Lat. *medietas*, Fr. *moitié*),
but always as it is used here, signifying 'a portion,' unless it may be
held to mean 'a third' in *1 Henry IV*, III, i, 96.

29. **royal merchant**. A complimentary phrase, to indicate the
wealth and social standing of Antonio. In Shakespeare's time, Sir
Thomas Gresham was so called, from his great wealth and from his
close financial relations with the court and the queen. The term
was also applied to great Italian merchants, such as the Giustiniani
and the Grimaldi, the Medici and the Pazzi, some of whom held
mortgages on kingdoms and acquired the titles of princes for themselves. Cf. the modern expression 'merchant prince.'

From stubborn Turks and Tartars, never train'd
To offices of tender courtesy.
We all expect a gentle answer, Jew.   34

    SHYLOCK. I have possess'd your Grace of what I purpose ;
And by our holy Sabbath have I sworn
To have the due and forfeit of my bond :
If you deny it, let the danger light
Upon your charter and your city's freedom.
You 'll ask me, why I rather choose to have   40
A weight of carrion-flesh than to receive
Three thousand ducats : I 'll not answer that :
But, say, it is my humour ; is it answer'd ?
What if my house be troubl'd with a rat,
And I be pleas'd to give ten thousand ducats   45
To have it ban'd ! What, are you answer'd yet ?
Some men there are love not a gaping pig ;

   35. SHYLOCK | Jew QqFf.   36. Sabbath Q1Ff | Sabaoth Q2.

   34. Here, as in II, vi, 51, there may be a pun on 'gentle.'

   35. possess'd : informed fully. So in I, iii, 60.

   39. Perhaps Shakespeare had London in his mind, which held
certain rights and franchises by royal charter, and was liable to have
its charter revoked for an act of flagrant injustice.

   43. The meaning seems to be : What if I should say it is my
humor ; is that an answer ? In the Elizabethan time humor was
used, much as conscience was at a later period, to justify any eccen-
tric impulse for which no ground of reason could be alleged. Thus,
if a man had an individual crotchet which he meant should over-
ride the laws and conditions of our social being, it was his humor.

   46. ban'd : poisoned. Cf. *Measure for Measure*, I, ii, 133.

   47. A pig's head as roasted for the table. In England a boar's
head was served up at Christmas with a lemon in its mouth. So in
Webster's *Duchess of Malfi*, III, ii : " He could not abide to see
a pig's head gaping : I thought your grace would find him a Jew."
And in Fletcher's *Elder Brother*, II, ii, "Gaping like a roasted pig."

Some, that are mad if they behold a cat;
And others, when the bag-pipe sings i' the nose.
Masters of passion sways it to the mood   50
Of what it likes or loathes. Now, for your answer :
As there is no firm reason to be render'd,
Why he cannot abide a gaping pig;
Why he, a harmless necessary cat;
Why he, a woollen bag-pipe, but of force   55
Must yield to such inevitable shame
As to offend, himself being offended;
So can I give no reason, nor I will not,
More than a lodg'd hate and a certain loathing
I bear Antonio, that I follow thus   60
A losing suit against him. Are you answer'd?

50. **sways.** For discussion of third person plural in *-s*, see Abbott,
§ 333. — **it.** Passion.

51. **of what it likes or loathes.** An axiomatic saying. Even the
greatest masters of passion move and rule it according as it is pre-
disposed. Shakespeare's power lies partly in that fact: hence, in
his work, the passions are rooted in the persons, instead of being
merely pasted on. Grant White suggests that 'masters of passion'
may refer to "those things or occurrences (such as the instances just
cited by Shylock) that move either the sympathy or antipathy of
any man."

55. **a woollen bag-pipe.** Bagpipes used to be carried or kept in
woolen cases. Johnson proposed 'wooden,' and Sir John Hawkins
'swollen'; which latter Steevens adopted. Collier's Second Folio
has 'bollen,' which is an old word meaning about the same as
'swollen'; and Dyce adopts that reading. 'Wauling' is Capell's
conjecture; and both Dr. Ingleby and Mr. A. E. Brae, each inde-
pendently of the other, and without being aware of Capell's conjecture, hit upon the same correction. Mason notes that it is not
by the sight of the bagpipe that persons are affected, but by the
sound.

BASSANIO.   This is no answer, thou unfeeling man,
To excuse the current of thy cruelty.   63

SHYLOCK.   I am not bound to please thee with my answer.

BASSANIO.   Do all men kill the things they do not love?

SHYLOCK.   Hates any man the thing he would not kill?

BASSANIO.   Every offence is not a hate at first.   67

SHYLOCK.   What, wouldst thou have a serpent sting thee
        twice?

ANTONIO.   I pray you, think you question with the Jew.
You may as well go stand upon the beach,   70
And bid the main flood bate his usual height;
You may as well use question with the wolf,
Why he hath made the ewe bleat for the lamb;
You may as well forbid the mountain pines
To wag their high tops, and to make no noise,   75
When they are fretted with the gusts of heaven;
You may as well do anything most hard,
As seek to soften that — than which what's harder? —
His Jewish heart: therefore, I do beseech you,
Make no more offers, use no further means;   80
But with all brief and plain conveniency
Let me have judgment, and the Jew his will.

---

72. **You may** Qq | Or even Ff.
73. **Why he hath made the ewe
bleat for the lamb**: Q₃Q₄ | Why he
hath made the ewe bleake for the
Lambe: Q₁ | The ewe bleate for

the Lambe: F₁ | The ewe bleate for
the Lambe: when you behold, F₂
F₃F₄ Rowe.
76. **fretted** Ff | fretten Qq.
78. **what's** Qq | what F₁F₂F₃.

69. "Remember you are arguing with Shylock, whose cruel nature
is known." — Clar.

71. **main flood**: ocean tide. — **bate**: lessen, reduce.

81. **brief and plain conveniency**: convenient brevity and plainness.

82. Let the sentence proceed against me with such promptness
and directness as befit the administration of justice.

BASSANIO. For thy three thousand ducats here is six.

SHYLOCK. If every ducat in six thousand ducats
Were in six parts, and every part a ducat,   85
I would not draw them; I would have my bond.

DUKE. How shalt thou hope for mercy, rendering none?

SHYLOCK. What judgment shall I dread, doing no wrong?
You have among you many a purchas'd slave,
Which, like your asses and your dogs and mules,   90
You use in abject and in slavish parts,
Because you bought them: shall I say to you,
Let them be free, marry them to your heirs?
Why sweat they under burthens? let their beds
Be made as soft as yours, and let their palates   95
Be season'd with such viands? You will answer,
'The slaves are ours.'—So do I answer you:
The pound of flesh, which I demand of him,
Is dearly bought; 't is mine, and I will have it.
If you deny me, fie upon your law!   100
There is no force in the decrees of Venice.
I stand for judgment: answer; shall I have it?

DUKE. Upon my power I may dismiss this court,
Unless Bellario, a learned doctor,
Whom I have sent for to determine this,   105
Come here to-day.

SALERIO.   My lord, here stays without
A messenger with letters from the doctor,
New come from Padua.

DUKE. Bring us the letters; call the messenger.   109

BASSANIO. Good cheer, Antonio! What, man, courage yet!

---

106. SALERIO Q2 | Saler. Q1 | Sal.   109. **messenger** Qq | messengers
Ff.   Ff.

The Jew shall have my flesh, blood, bones, and all,
Ere thou shalt lose for me one drop of blood.

ANTONIO.   I am a tainted wether of the flock,
Meetest for death : the weakest kind of fruit
Drops earliest to the ground ; and so let me :   115
You cannot better be employ'd, Bassanio,
Than to live still, and write mine epitaph.

Enter NERISSA, *dressed like a lawyer's clerk*

DUKE.   Came you from Padua, from Bellario?

NERISSA.   From both, my lord.   Bellario greets your Grace.
                                [*Presenting a letter*]

BASSANIO.   Why dost thou whet thy knife so earnestly?

SHYLOCK.   To cut the forfeiture from that bankrupt there.

GRATIANO.   Not on thy sole, but on thy soul, harsh Jew,
Thou mak'st thy knife keen ; but no metal can,   123
No, not the hangman's axe, bear half the keenness
Of thy sharp envy.   Can no prayers pierce thee?

SHYLOCK.   No, none that thou hast wit enough to make.

GRATIANO.   O, be thou damn'd, inexecrable dog !
And for thy life let justice be accus'd.
Thou almost mak'st me waver in my faith,
To hold opinion with Pythagoras,   130

112. lose Q1 | loose Q2F1F2F3.   my L. Q1 | both. My Lord (two lines)
118. Scene II Pope. — *dressed* Ff.
. . . *clerk* Rowe | omitted in Ff.   127. inexecrable QqF1F2 | inexor-
119. both, my lord. Camb | both,   able F3F4.

127. inexecrable : "that cannot be execrated enough." — Clar.
128. Let justice be impeached or arraigned for suffering thee to live.
130. Pythagoras. The ancient philosopher of Samos, who is said
to have held the doctrine of transmigration of souls. Shakespeare
has two other famous references to him and his tenets : *As You Like
It*, III, ii, 187, and *Twelfth Night*, IV, ii, 53–65.

That souls of animals infuse themselves
Into the trunks of men : thy currish spirit
Govern'd a wolf, who, hang'd for human slaughter,
Even from the gallows did his fell soul fleet,
And, whilst thou lay'st in thy unhallow'd dam,   135
Infus'd itself in thee ; for thy desires
Are wolfish, bloody, starv'd, and ravenous.

    SHYLOCK. Till thou canst rail the seal from off my bond,
Thou but offend'st thy lungs to speak so loud :
Repair thy wit, good youth, or it will fall   140
To cureless ruin. I stand here for law.

    DUKE. This letter from Bellario doth commend
A young and learned doctor to our court. —
Where is he?

    NERISSA.   He attendeth here hard by,
To know your answer, whether you 'll admit him.   145

    DUKE. With all my heart. — Some three or four of you
Go give him courteous conduct to this place. —
Meantime the court shall hear Bellario's letter.   148

    CLERK. [*Reads*]

Your Grace shall understand, that at the receipt of your letter
I am very sick : but in the instant that your messenger came,
in loving visitation was with me a young doctor of Rome ; his
name is Balthasar. I acquainted him with the cause in contro-
versy between the Jew and Antonio the merchant : we turn'd
o'er many books together : he is furnish'd with my opinion ;
which, better'd with his own learning, — the greatness whereof

---

    141. cureless Qq | endless Ff | 143. to Qq | in Ff.
careless Pope.   149. CLERK. [*Reads*] | QqFf omit.

    133. who, hang'd. Nominative absolute. See Abbott, § 376.
    139. to speak : in speaking. Infinitives used indefinitely. See
Abbott, § 356.

I cannot enough commend, — comes with him, at my impor-
tunity, to fill up your Grace's request in my stead. I beseech
you, let his lack of years be no impediment to let him lack a
reverend estimation; for I never knew so young a body with so
old a head. I leave him to your gracious acceptance, whose
trial shall better publish his commendation.   161

DUKE. You hear the learn'd Bellario, what he writes:
And here, I take it, is the doctor come. —

Enter PORTIA, *dressed like a doctor of laws*

Give me your hand. Come you from old Bellario?
    PORTIA. I did, my lord.
    DUKE.   You are welcome: take your place.
Are you acquainted with the difference   166
That holds this present question in the court?
    PORTIA. I am informed throughly of the cause.
Which is the merchant here, and which the Jew?
    DUKE. Antonio and old Shylock, both stand forth.   170
    PORTIA. Is your name Shylock?
    SHYLOCK.   Shylock is my name.
    PORTIA. Of a strange nature is the suit you follow;
Yet in such rule, that the Venetian law

161. After this line in QqFf 'En-   164. *Enter* . . . | Enter Portia
ter Portia for Balthasar' (Balthazer   Dress'd like a Doctor of Laws Rowe.
Q1Q2 | Balthazar F1F2).   164. Come Qq | Came Ff.

158–159. Let his youthfulness be no hindrance to his being rever-
ently esteemed. Professor Gummere suggests that 'let him lack'
may be a printer's repetition of 'let his lack'; but as the text stands
the play upon words is thoroughly Shakespearian.
    160. whose: for his. See Abbott, § 263.
    167. question. The dispute to decide which the present inquiry
is held.

Cannot impugn you as you do proceed. —
You stand within his danger, do you not?   175
   ANTONIO. Ay, so he says.
   PORTIA.   Do you confess the bond?
   ANTONIO. I do.
   PORTIA.   Then must the Jew be merciful.
   SHYLOCK. On what compulsion must I? tell me that.
   PORTIA. The quality of mercy is not strain'd ;
It droppeth as the gentle rain from heaven   180
Upon the place beneath : it is twice blest ;
It blesseth him that gives, and him that takes :
'T is mightiest in the mightiest : it becomes
The throned monarch better than his crown ;
His sceptre shows the force of temporal power,   185
The attribute to awe and majesty,

---

175. "Within one's danger" properly meant within some one's power or control, liable to a penalty which he might impose. Sometimes, however, it was used for being in some one's debt. Here the meaning seems to be, Your life is in his power, and so in danger from him. See Skeat for history of the word 'danger.'

179. The nature of mercy is to act freely, not from constraint. Portia had used 'must' in a moral sense, and the Jew purposely took it in a legal sense. This gives a natural occasion and impulse for her strain of "heavenly eloquence."

183. This may mean, either that mercy exists in the greatest plenitude in Him who is omnipotent, or that the more power one has to inflict pain, the more one bows and subdues the heart by showing mercy. If the former, it should be printed "in the Mightiest." It was evidently a favorite idea with Shakespeare that the noblest and most amiable thing is power mixed with gentleness; and that the highest style of manhood is that which knows no fear of pain, but is a child to the touches of compassion.

186. The thing attributed or assigned for the purpose of inspiring awe and of symbolizing majesty.

Wherein doth sit the dread and fear of kings;
But mercy is above this sceptred sway;
It is enthroned in the hearts of kings,
It is an attribute to God himself;   190
And earthly power doth then show likest God's
When mercy seasons justice. Therefore, Jew,
Though justice be thy plea, consider this,—
That, in the course of justice, none of us
Should see salvation: we do pray for mercy;   195
And that same prayer doth teach us all to render
The deeds of mercy. I have spoke thus much
To mitigate the justice of thy plea;
Which if thou follow, this strict court of Venice
Must needs give sentence 'gainst the merchant there.   200

SHYLOCK. My deeds upon my head! I crave the law,
The penalty and forfeit of my bond.

PORTIA. Is he not able to discharge the money?

BASSANIO. Yes, here I tender it for him in the court;
Yea, twice the sum: if that will not suffice,   205
I will be bound to pay it ten times o'er,
On forfeit of my hands, my head, my heart:

191. likest Q2Ff | lik'st Q1.   199. court Qq | course Ff.

196. "Portia, referring the Jew to the Christian doctrine of salvation, and the Lord's Prayer, is a little out of character." So
says Judge Blackstone; whereas the Lord's Prayer was itself but a
compilation, all the petitions in it being taken out of the ancient
euchologies or prayer books of the Jews. So in *Ecclesiasticus*,
xxviii, 2: "Forgive thy neighbour the hurt that he hath done unto
thee, so shall thy sins also be forgiven when thou prayest."

205. twice. In previous editions of Hudson's Shakespeare the
reading 'thrice' was followed to bring the statement into exact
agreement with that in ll. 222, 229, but in Shakespeare there are
many slips of this kind.

If this will not suffice, it must appear
That malice bears down truth. And I beseech you,
Wrest once the law to your authority :   210
To do a great right, do a little wrong ;
And curb this cruel devil of his will.

PORTIA. It must not be ; there is no power in Venice
Can alter a decree established :
'T will be recorded for a precedent ;   215
And many an error, by the same example,
Will rush into the state. It cannot be.

SHYLOCK. A Daniel come to judgment ! yea, a Daniel !
O wise young judge, how I do honour thee !

PORTIA. I pray you, let me look upon the bond.   220

SHYLOCK. Here 't is, most reverend doctor ; here it is.

PORTIA. Shylock, there 's thrice thy money offer'd thee.

SHYLOCK. An oath, an oath, I have an oath in heaven :
Shall I lay perjury upon my soul?
No, not for Venice.

PORTIA.   Why, this bond is forfeit ;   225
And lawfully by this the Jew may claim
A pound of flesh, to be by him cut off
Nearest the merchant's heart. — Be merciful ;
Take thrice thy money ; bid me tear the bond.

SHYLOCK. When it is paid according to the tenour.   230
It doth appear you are a worthy judge ;

---

215. precedent Qq | President Ff.   219. I do Qq | do I Ff.

209. truth : honesty. A 'true' man in old language is an 'honest'
man. The honesty here is in offering to pay thrice the money.

218. Daniel. See *The History of Susanna* and *Bel and the Dragon*
in the Apocrypha. Cf. also *Ezekiel*, xxviii, 3 ; *Daniel*, vi, 3.

230. tenour. 'Tenure' is the Folio spelling.

You know the law, your exposition
Hath been most sound : I charge you by the law,
Whereof you are a well-deserving pillar,
Proceed to judgment. By my soul I swear   235
There is no power in the tongue of man
To alter me : I stay here on my bond.

ANTONIO. Most heartily I do beseech the court
To give the judgment.

PORTIA.   Why then, thus it is :
You must prepare your bosom for his knife.   240

SHYLOCK. O noble judge ! O excellent young man !

PORTIA. For the intent and purpose of the law
Hath full relation to the penalty,
Which here appeareth due upon the bond.

SHYLOCK. 'T is very true. O wise and upright judge ! 245
How much more elder art thou than thy looks !

PORTIA. Therefore lay bare your bosom.

SHYLOCK.   Ay, his breast :
So says the bond : — doth it not, noble judge ? —
Nearest his heart : those are the very words.

PORTIA. It is so. Are there balance here to weigh   250
The flesh ?

SHYLOCK. I have them ready.

---

247. your QqF₁F₂F₃ | thy F₄.   250-251. Printed as prose in QqFf.

237. on : in dependence on. See Abbott, § 180.

242-243. The law relating to contracts is fully applicable in this case.

246. more elder. Double comparatives and superlatives are common in Shakespeare and Elizabethan literature generally. See Abbott, § 11.

250. balance. This singular form, due to the sibilant ending, is common in sixteenth century literature. So in Baret's *Alvearie* (1580) : "Balances, or a payre of balance."

PORTIA.   Have by some surgeon, Shylock, on your charge,
To stop his wounds, lest he do bleed to death.

SHYLOCK.   Is it so nominated in the bond?

PORTIA.   It is not so express'd; but what of that?   255
'T were good you do so much for charity.

SHYLOCK.   I cannot find it; 't is not in the bond.

PORTIA.   Come, merchant, have you any thing to say?

ANTONIO.   But little: I am arm'd and well prepar'd. —
Give me your hand, Bassanio: fare you well!   260
Grieve not that I am fall'n to this for you;
For herein Fortune shows herself more kind
Than is her custom: it is still her use
To let the wretched man outlive his wealth,
To view with hollow eye and wrinkled brow   265
An age of poverty; from which lingering penance
Of such a misery doth she cut me off.
Commend me to your honourable wife:
Tell her the process of Antonio's end;
Say how I lov'd you, speak me fair in death;   270
And, when the tale is told, bid her be judge
Whether Bassanio had not once a love.
Repent not you that you shall lose your friend,
And he repents not that he pays your debt;
For, if the Jew do cut but deep enough,   275
I'll pay it instantly with all my heart.

253. **do** Qq | should Ff.   267. such a $F_2F_3F_4$ | such QqF1.
254. **Is it so** Qq | It is not Ff.   273. **not you** Ff | but you Qq.
258. **Come** Ff | you Qq.   276. **instantly** Q_2Ff | presently Q1.

263. **still her use**: ever her custom. See note, p. 4, l. 17.

270. "Speak well of me when I am dead." — Clar. Or, perhaps,
Tell the world that I died like a man.

276. An equivoque on 'heart'; and it rather heightens the pathos.

BASSANIO. Antonio, I am married to a wife
Which is as dear to me as life itself;
But life itself, my wife, and all the world,
Are not with me esteem'd above thy life: 280
I would lose all, ay, sacrifice them all
Here to this devil, to deliver you.

PORTIA. Your wife would give you little thanks for that,
If she were by, to hear you make the offer.

GRATIANO. I have a wife, whom, I protest, I love: 285
I would she were in heaven, so she could
Entreat some power to change this currish Jew.

NERISSA. 'T is well you offer it behind her back;
The wish would make else an unquiet house.

SHYLOCK. [Aside] These be the Christian husbands! I
     have a daughter;   290
Would any of the stock of Barrabas
Had been her husband rather than a Christian!
[Aloud] We trifle time: I pray thee, pursue sentence.

PORTIA. A pound of that same merchant's flesh is thine:
The court awards it, and the law doth give it.   295

SHYLOCK. Most rightful judge!

PORTIA. And you must cut this flesh from off his breast:
The law allows it, and the court awards it.

SHYLOCK. Most learned judge! A sentence! Come,
     prepare!

PORTIA. Tarry a little; there is something else.   300
This bond doth give thee here no jot of blood;

---

281. ay, Pope | I QqFf.   285. whom Ff | who Qq.

278. 'Which' for 'who.' A common usage. See Abbott, § 265.
291. **Barrabas.** Here, as with Barabas in *The Jew of Malta*, the
word is accented on the first syllable.

The words expressly are, a pound of flesh :
Take then thy bond, take thou thy pound of flesh ;
But, in the cutting it, if thou dost shed
One drop of Christian blood, thy lands and goods   305
Are, by the laws of Venice, confiscate
Unto the state of Venice.

    GRATIANO. O upright judge! Mark, Jew: O learned judge!

    SHYLOCK. Is that the law !

    PORTIA.   Thyself shalt see the act :
For, as thou urgest justice, be assur'd   310
Thou shalt have justice, more than thou desirest.

    GRATIANO. O learned judge!—Mark, Jew: a learned judge!

    SHYLOCK. I take this offer, then;—pay the bond thrice,
And let the Christian go.

    BASSANIO.   Here is the money.

    PORTIA. Soft !   315
The Jew shall have all justice ; soft ! no haste :
He shall have nothing but the penalty.

    GRATIANO. O Jew ! an upright judge, a learned judge !

    PORTIA. Therefore prepare thee to cut off the flesh.
Shed thou no blood ; nor cut thou less nor more   320
But just a pound of flesh : if thou cut'st more
Or less than a just pound, — be it but so much
As makes it light or heavy in the substance,
Or the division of the twentieth part
Of one poor scruple, nay, if the scale do turn   325
But in the estimation of a hair, —
Thou diest, and all thy goods are confiscate.

---

    303. **Take then** Qq | Then take
Ff.
    308. Two lines in QqFf.

    315-316. One line in QqFf.
    321. cut'st Q1 | tak'st Q2Ff.
    322. be it but Qq | be it Ff.

GRATIANO.   A second Daniel, a Daniel, Jew!
Now, infidel, I have thee on the hip.

PORTIA.   Why doth the Jew pause? take thy forfeiture.   330

SHYLOCK.   Give me my principal, and let me go.

BASSANIO.   I have it ready for thee; here it is.

PORTIA.   He hath refus'd it in the open court:
He shall have merely justice and his bond.

GRATIANO.   A Daniel, still say I, a second Daniel! —   335
I thank thee, Jew, for teaching me that word.

SHYLOCK.   Shall I not have barely my principal?

PORTIA.   Thou shalt have nothing but the forfeiture,
To be so taken at thy peril, Jew.

SHYLOCK.   Why, then the devil give him good of it!   340
I 'll stay no longer question.

PORTIA.   Tarry, Jew:
The law hath yet another hold on you.
It is enacted in the laws of Venice,
If it be proved against an alien
That by direct or indirect attempts   345
He seek the life of any citizen,
The party 'gainst the which he doth contrive
Shall seize one half his goods; the other half
Comes to the privy coffer of the state;
And the offender's life lies in the mercy   350
Of the Duke only, 'gainst all other voice.
In which predicament, I say, thou stand'st;
For it appears, by manifest proceeding,

---

329. thee Ff | you Qq.   341. question | here in question Q₁.
339. so taken Qq | taken so Ff.   348. one Q₂Ff | on Q₁.

330. In Furness is a suggestive note on this 'pause.'
352. predicament.   See Century for the history of this word.

That indirectly, and directly too,
Thou hast contriv'd against the very life   355
Of the defendant; and thou hast incurr'd
The danger formerly by me rehears'd.
Down, therefore, and beg mercy of the Duke.

GRATIANO. Beg that thou mayst have leave to hang thyself:
And yet, thy wealth being forfeit to the state,   360
Thou hast not left the value of a cord;
Therefore thou must be hang'd at the state's charge.

DUKE. That thou shalt see the difference of our spirits,
I pardon thee thy life before thou ask it:
For half thy wealth, it is Antonio's;   365
The other half comes to the general state,
Which humbleness may drive unto a fine.

PORTIA. Ay, for the state; not for Antonio.

SHYLOCK. Nay, take my life and all; pardon not that:
You take my house, when you do take the prop   370
That doth sustain my house; you take my life,
When you do take the means whereby I live.

PORTIA. What mercy can you render him, Antonio?

GRATIANO. A halter gratis; nothing else, for God's sake.

ANTONIO. So please my lord the Duke and all the court
To quit the fine for one half of his goods,   376
I am content; so he will let me have

355. hast QqF1 | had F2F3F4.   363. spirits Q1 | spirit Q2Ff.

367. Submission on your part may move me to reduce it to a fine.
368. Meaning, apparently, that the reduction of the forfeiture to
a fine should apply only to that half of his goods which was to come
to the coffer of the state, not to that which fell to Antonio.
376. If the court will remit the fine or acquit Shylock of the forfeiture so far as the claim of the state is concerned. Shakespeare
often uses 'quit' for 'acquit' or 'release.' Cf. *As You Like It*, III, i, 11.

The other half in use, to render it,
Upon his death, unto the gentleman
That lately stole his daughter :   380
Two things provided more, — that, for this favour,
He presently become a Christian ;
The other, that he do record a gift,
Here in the court, of all he dies possess'd,
Unto his son Lorenzo and his daughter.   385

    DUKE. He shall do this ; or else I do recant
The pardon that I late pronounced here.

    PORTIA. Art thou contented, Jew ? what dost thou say ?

    SHYLOCK. I am content.

    PORTIA.   Clerk, draw a deed of gift.

    SHYLOCK, I pray you, give me leave to go from hence ; 390
I am not well : send the deed after me,
And I will sign it.

    DUKE.   Get thee gone, but do it.

    GRATIANO. In christening shalt thou have two godfathers :

---

389. **Clerk** | Clearke Q1 | Clarke F1.   393. **shalt thou** Qq | thou shalt Ff.

378. " That is, in trust for Shylock during his life, for the purpose
of securing it at his (not 'my,' as suggested by Johnson) death to
Lorenzo. . . .   In conveyances of land, where it is intended to give
the estate to any person after the death of another, it is necessary
that a third person should be possessed of the estate, and the use
be declared to the one after the death of the other, or the estate
to the future possessor would be rendered insecure.   This is called
a conveyance to uses."   The anonymous author of the foregoing,
cited by Halliwell, adds that Shakespeare has rendered the old Latin
law phrase pertaining to the case " with all the strictness of a tech-
nical conveyancer, and has made Antonio desire to have one half
of Shylock's goods in *use*, — to render it upon his (Shylock's) death
to Lorenzo — not an unfrequent mode of securing a future estate."

382. **presently** : at once.   So below in l. 399 and l. 450.

Had I been judge, thou shouldst have had ten more,
To bring thee to the gallows, not the font. [*Exit* SHYLOCK]

    DUKE.   Sir, I entreat you home with me to dinner.   396

    PORTIA.   I humbly do desire your Grace of pardon :
I must away this night toward Padua,
And it is meet I presently set forth.

    DUKE.   I am sorry that your leisure serves you not. — 400
Antonio, gratify this gentleman ;
For, in my mind, you are much bound to him.

                [*Exeunt the* DUKE *and his train*]

    BASSANIO.   Most worthy gentleman, I and my friend
Have by your wisdom been this day acquitted
Of grievous penalties ; in lieu whereof,   405
Three thousand ducats, due unto the Jew,
We freely cope your courteous pains withal.

    ANTONIO.   And stand indebted, over and above,
In love and service to you evermore.

    PORTIA.   He is well paid that is well satisfied ;   410
And I, delivering you, am satisfied,
And therein do account myself well paid :
My mind was never yet more mercenary.
I pray you, know me when we meet again :
I wish you well, and so I take my leave.   415

---

    395. not the Q1 | not to the Q2Ff   **396.** home with me Qq | with me
Q3Q4.   home Ff.

    394. Meaning a jury of twelve men to condemn him. This appears
to have been an old joke, and is found in Ben Jonson.

    397. An English idiom now obsolete. So in *A Midsummer Night's
Dream*, III, i, 185 : "I shall desire you of more acquaintance."

    401. gratify : recompense. Cf. *Coriolanus*, II, ii, 44.

    407. cope : reward, requite. — **withal.** A preposition governing
'ducats.' See Abbott, § 196.

BASSANIO. Dear sir, of force I must attempt you further:
Take some remembrance of us, as a tribute,
Not as a fee: grant me two things, I pray you,
Not to deny me, and to pardon me.   419

PORTIA. You press me far, and therefore I will yield. —
[*To* ANTONIO] Give me your gloves, I 'll wear them for your
        sake ; —
[*To* BASSANIO] And, for your love, I 'll take this ring from you.
Do not draw back your hand ; I 'll take no more ;
And you in love shall not deny me this.

BASSANIO. This ring, good sir, — alas, it is a trifle !   425
I will not shame myself to give you this.

PORTIA. I will have nothing else but only this ;
And now methinks I have a mind to it.

BASSANIO. There 's more depends on this than on the value.
The dearest ring in Venice will I give you,   430
And find it out by proclamation :
Only for this, I pray you, pardon me.

PORTIA. I see, sir, you are liberal in offers :
You taught me first to beg ; and now methinks
You teach me how a beggar should be answer'd.   435

---

418. a fee Q1F2 | fee Q2F1.   424. this. Q1 | this? Q2F1.

416. attempt: tempt. Cf. *Measure for Measure*, IV, ii, 205.
429. The First Quarto reads :

        There 's more then this depends upon the valew.

The First Folio :

        There 's more depends on this then on the valew.

Theobald's conjecture is :

        There 's more depends on this, than is the value.

Capell suggests :

        There 's more depends on this than the stone's value.

BASSANIO.   Good sir, this ring was given me by my wife ;
And when she put it on, she made me vow
That I should neither sell nor give nor lose it.

PORTIA.   That 'scuse serves many men to save their gifts.
And if your wife be not a mad-woman,   440
And know how well I have deserv'd this ring,
She would not hold out enemy for ever
For giving it to me. Well, peace be with you !

> [*Exeunt* PORTIA *and* NERISSA]

ANTONIO.   My Lord Bassanio, let him have the ring :
Let his deservings, and my love withal,   445
Be valued 'gainst your wife's commandment.

BASSANIO.   Go, Gratiano, run and overtake him ;
Give him the ring ; and bring him, if thou canst,
Unto Antonio's house. Away ! make haste. —

> [*Exit* GRATIANO]

Come, you and I will thither presently ;   450
And in the morning early will we both
Fly toward Belmont : come, Antonio.   [*Exeunt*]

SCENE II.   *The same. A street*

Enter PORTIA *and* NERISSA

PORTIA.   Inquire the Jew's house out, give him this deed,
And let him sign it : we 'll away to-night,

441. this ring Q₂Ff | the ring Q₁.   446. 'gainst Q₃ | gainst Q₁ | against Ff.

446. **commandment.** Properly four syllables here, as if written
'commandement.' And so, in fact, it is spelled in the Quartos
('commaundement,' Second Quarto) and the first three Folios. Perhaps the old spelling should in such cases be retained, as in the metrical version of the *Psalms* still used in the Presbyterian churches
of Scotland.

And be a day before our husbands home.
This deed will be well welcome to Lorenzo.

Enter GRATIANO

GRATIANO.   Fair sir, you are well o'erta'en :   5
My Lord Bassanio, upon more advice,
Hath sent you here this ring, and doth entreat
Your company at dinner.

PORTIA.   That cannot be :
His ring I do accept most thankfully ;
And so, I pray you, tell him : furthermore,   10
I pray you, show my youth old Shylock's house.

GRATIANO.   That will I do.

NERISSA.   Sir, I would speak with you.—
[*Aside to* PORTIA] I 'll see if I can get my husband's ring,
Which I did make him swear to keep for ever.

PORTIA. [*Aside to* NERISSA] Thou mayst, I warrant. We
          shall have old swearing   15
That they did give the rings away to men ;
But we 'll outface them, and outswear them too.
Away ! make haste : thou know'st where I will tarry.

NERISSA.   Come, good sir ; will you show me to this house ?
                                        [*Exeunt*]

13, 15. [*Aside . . .*] omitted in QqFf.   9. **His ring** Q2Ff | This ring Q1.

6. **advice** : consideration. Cf. 'advised' in I, i, 142.

15. **old.** A frequent intensive in colloquial speech in the sixteenth
century, and reappearing in the twentieth in slang expressions and
street and college songs. So in *Much Ado About Nothing*, V, ii, 98 :
" Yonder 's old coil at home." And in *The Merry Wives of Windsor*,
I, iv, 5 : " here will be an old abusing of God's patience and the
king's English."

ACT V

SCENE I. *Belmont. Avenue to* PORTIA'S *house*

Enter LORENZO *and* JESSICA

LORENZO. The moon shines bright. In such a night as this,
When the sweet wind did gently kiss the trees,
And they did make no noise, — in such a night
Troilus methinks mounted the Troyan walls,
And sigh'd his soul toward the Grecian tents,   5
Where Cressid lay that night.

JESSICA.   In such a night
Did Thisbe fearfully o'ertrip the dew,
And saw the lion's shadow ere himself,
And ran dismay'd away.

Avenue to . . . Capell | A Grove
or Green Place before . . . Theobald.
1. Printed in two lines Q1.

4. **Troilus** | Troylus F1.— **Troyan**
Q1 | Troian F1 | Trojan Q3. — **walls**
QqF1 | wall F2F3F4.
6. **Cressid** | Cressed F1 | Cressada
Q1.

4. The story of Troilus and Cressida is dramatized in Shakespeare's play of that name. This development of the Troy-legend is probably the invention of Benoît de Sainte-More, a twelfth century trouvère. Benoît's 'Briseida' became 'Griseida' in Boccaccio's *Il Filostrato*, and 'Criseyde' in Chaucer's version of the story. Line 666, Book V, of Chaucer's *Troilus and Criseyde* may have suggested the passage in Lorenzo's speech.

7. The story of "Pyramus and his love Thisbe" is burlesqued in the interlude of Bottom and company in *A Midsummer Night's Dream*. In Chaucer's *The Legend of Good Women* the stories of Thisbe, Dido, and Medea follow one another in the same order as here.

LORENZO.   In such a night
Stood Dido with a willow in her hand   10
Upon the wild sea banks, and waft her love
To come again to Carthage.

JESSICA.   In such a night
Medea gather'd the enchanted herbs
That did renew old Æson.

LORENZO.   In such a night
Did Jessica steal from the wealthy Jew,   15
And with an unthrift love did run from Venice
As far as Belmont.

JESSICA.   In such a night
Did young Lorenzo swear he lov'd her well,
Stealing her soul with many vows of faith,
And ne'er a true one.

LORENZO.   In such a night   20
Did pretty Jessica, like a little shrew,
Slander her love, and he forgave it her.

11. waft QqFf | wav'd Theobald.   21. shrew Q1 | shrow Q2Ff.

10. Spenser in like sort makes the willow a symbol of forsaken
love. So in *The Faerie Queene*, I, i, 9. In ll. 10–12, as also in ll. 1–4,
Matthew Arnold says "we have the sheer, inimitable Celtic note."

11. waft: wafted. See Abbott, § 341.

13. Twice before in this play we have had allusions to the story
of Jason and his voyage to Colchis (Colchos, I, i, 171) in quest of
the golden fleece. Medea, daughter of the King of Colchis, fell
in love with Jason and helped him to win the fleece; then, having
stolen her father's treasure, ran away with her lover to Greece.
Jason's father was very old and infirm; and Medea, by a broth of
magic herbs, renewed the old man's youth. In Ovid (*Metamorphoses*,
VII; Golding's translation, 1567) the sorceress gathers the herbs by
moonlight; in Gower (*Confessio Amantis*, V), by starlight. Medea's
elopement suggests Jessica's own story to Lorenzo.

JESSICA. I would out-night you, did no body come :
But, hark, I hear the footing of a man.

Enter STEPHANO

LORENZO. Who comes so fast in silence of the night? 25
STEPHANO. A friend.
LORENZO. A friend ! what friend ? your name, I pray you,
    friend ?
STEPHANO. Stephano is my name ; and I bring word
My mistress will before the break of day
Be here at Belmont : she doth stray about   30
By holy crosses, where she kneels and prays
For happy wedlock hours.
LORENZO.   Who comes with her?
STEPHANO. None but a holy hermit and her maid.
I pray you, is my master yet return'd?   34
LORENZO. He is not, nor we have not heard from him. —
But go we in, I pray thee, Jessica,
And ceremoniously let us prepare
Some welcome for the mistress of the house.   38

23. no body Q2Ff | nobody Q1.   Enter a Messenger Qq | Enter Mes-
24. *Enter* STEPHANO Theobald | senger Ff.

28. In this play the name Stephano has the accent on the second
syllable. In *The Tempest* the same name has it, rightly, on the
first.

31. In old times crosses such as are still to be seen by the traveler
in southern Europe were set up at the intersection of roads, and in
other places especially associated with saintly or heroic names, to
invite the passers-by to devotion. And in those days Christians were
much in the habit of remembering in their prayers whatever lay
nearest their hearts. Shakespeare expresses the same old thought
still more sweetly in two other places.

Enter LAUNCELOT

LAUNCELOT. Sola, sola! wo, ha, ho! sola, sola!

LORENZO. Who calls?   40

LAUNCELOT. Sola! did you see Master Lorenzo? Master
Lorenzo, sola, sola!

LORENZO. Leave hollaing, man: here.

LAUNCELOT. Sola! where? where?

LORENZO. Here.   45

LAUNCELOT. Tell him there's a post come from my master, with his horn full of good news: my master will be
here ere morning.   [*Exit*]

LORENZO. Sweet soul, let's in, and there expect their
        coming.

And yet no matter: why should we go in? —   50

My friend Stephano, signify, I pray you,

Within the house, your mistress is at hand;

And bring your music forth into the air.—[*Exit* STEPHANO]

How sweet the moonlight sleeps upon this bank!

Here will we sit, and let the sounds of music   55

Creep in our ears: soft stillness and the night

Become the touches of sweet harmony.

---

39. *Enter* LAUNCELOT Rowe |
Enter Clowne QqFf.

41-42. **Master Lorenzo? Master Lo-
renzo** Camb | M. Lorenzo, & M. Lo-
renzo Q₂F₁ | M. Lorenzo, M. Loren-
zo Q₁ | M. Lorenzo, and M. Lorenza
F₂ | M.Lorenzo and Mrs.Lorenza F₃.

49. LORENZO. **Sweet soul, let's in**
Malone | LOR. Sweet love, let's in
Rowe | sweete soule. LOREN. Let's
in QqF₁ | sweet love. LOR. Let's
in F₂.

51. **Stephano** Q₁F₂ | Stephen F₁.
—I omitted in F₁.

39. Launcelot sportively imitates the horn, referred to punningly
in l. 47, with which the 'post' used to herald his approach.

41-42. Furness humorously describes the evolution of the First
Folio text into the 'Master Lorenzo and Mistress Lorenzo' of
modern editors.

49. **expect**: await. So in Milton, *Paradise Lost*, XII, 591.

Sit, Jessica. Look, how the floor of heaven
Is thick inlaid with patens of bright gold :
There 's not the smallest orb which thou behold'st   60
But in his motion like an angel sings,
Still quiring to the young-eyed cherubins :
Such harmony is in immortal souls ;
But, whilst this muddy vesture of decay
Doth grossly close it in, we cannot hear it. —   65

Enter Musicians

Come, ho, and wake Diana with a hymn !
With sweetest touches pierce your mistress' ear,
And draw her home with music.   [*Music*]

59. **patens** | pattens Q2F1 | pattents   65. **close** it in Q2 | close in it
Q1 | patterns F2 | patines Malone.   Q1 Ff | close us in Rowe.

59. **patens** : small plates, commonly of gold or silver-gilt, used in
the celebration of the Eucharist. 'Patin,' 'patine' are obsolete forms
of the same word. Furness thinks the reference is to broken clouds,
bright in the moonlight ; but l. 60 undoubtedly refers to the stars.

60–63. " The music of the spheres " is an ancient mystery which
taught that the heavenly bodies in their revolutions sing together in
a concert so loud, various, and sweet as to exceed all proportion to
the human ear. And the greatest souls, from Plato (*Republic*, X) to
Wordsworth, have been lifted above themselves, with the idea that
the universe was knit together by a principle of which musical harmony is the aptest and clearest expression. Milton touches it with
surpassing sweetness in the morning hymn of Adam and Eve, *Paradise Lost*, V, 177, and also in *Arcades*, 62 ff. See also Coleridge's
Remorse, III, i, and Wordsworth's poem *On the Power of Sound*,
xii. Cf. *Job*, xxxviii, 7 : " The morning stars sang together."

63. So in Hooker's *Ecclesiastical Polity*, V, xxxviii : " Touching
musical harmony, such is the force thereof, and so pleasing effects
it hath in that very part of man which is most divine, that some
have thereby been induced to think that the soul itself by nature
is or hath in it harmony."

JESSICA.   I am never merry when I hear sweet music.

LORENZO.   The reason is, your spirits are attentive :   70
For do but note a wild and wanton herd,
Or race of youthful and unhandled colts,
Fetching mad bounds, bellowing and neighing loud,
Which is the hot condition of their blood ;
If they but hear perchance a trumpet sound,   75
Or any air of music touch their ears,
You shall perceive them make a mutual stand,
Their savage eyes turn'd to a modest gaze,
By the sweet power of music : therefore the poet
Did feign that Orpheus drew trees, stones, and floods ;   80
Since nought so stockish, hard, and full of rage,
But music for the time doth change his nature.
The man that hath no music in himself,
Nor is not mov'd with concord of sweet sounds,
Is fit for treasons, stratagems, and spoils ;   85
The motions of his spirit are dull as night,
And his affections dark as Erebus :
Let no such man be trusted.   Mark the music.

75. but hear perchance Q2Ff | perchance but hear Q1.

80. trees QqF1 | tears F2F3F4.
82. his QqF2 | omitted in F1.

79. Ovid, *Metamorphoses*, X, xi, tells this story of Orpheus.

87. Erebus : the darkest and gloomiest region of Hades.

88. Upon the general subject of this splendid strain touching music and musical harmony, it seems but just to quote a passage hardly inferior from Sir Thomas Browne, *Religio Medici*, II, ix: "There is a music wherever there is a harmony, order, or proportion ; and thus far we may maintain the music of the spheres: for those well-ordered motions and regular paces, though they give no sound unto the ear, yet to the understanding they strike a note most full of harmony. Whatsoever is harmonically composed delights in harmony ; which makes me much distrust the symmetry

Enter PORTIA *and* NERISSA

PORTIA.   That light we see is burning in my hall.
How far that little candle throws his beams !   90
So shines a good deed in a naughty world.

   NERISSA. When the moon shone, we did not see the candle.

   PORTIA.   So doth the greater glory dim the less :
A substitute shines brightly as a king,
Until a king be by ; and then his state   95
Empties itself, as doth an inland brook
Into the main of waters. Music ! hark !

   NERISSA.   It is your music, madam, of the house.

   PORTIA.   Nothing is good, I see, without respect :
Methinks it sounds much sweeter than by day.   100

   NERISSA.   Silence bestows that virtue on it, madam.

   PORTIA.   The crow doth sing as sweetly as the lark,
When neither is attended ; and I think

of those heads which declaim against all church-music. For myself,
not only from my obedience but my particular genius I do embrace
it : for even that vulgar and tavern music which makes one man
merry, another mad, strikes in me a deep fit of devotion, and a profound contemplation of the First Composer. There is something in
it of divinity more than the ear discovers ; it is an hieroglyphical
and shadowed lesson of the whole world and creatures of God, —
such a melody to the ear as the whole world, well understood, would
afford the understanding. In brief, it is a sensible fit of that harmony which intellectually sounds in the ears of God. I will not say,
with Plato, the soul is an harmony, but harmonical, and hath its
nearest sympathy unto music."

   99. Nothing is good unless it be regarded, heeded, or attended to.
Hence the music sounds much better when there is nothing to dis-
tract or divert the attention. This explanation is justified by what
Portia says in the second speech after.

   103. attended : heeded. Furness would take 'attended' literally.

The nightingale, if she should sing by day,
When every goose is cackling, would be thought   105
No better a musician than the wren.
How many things by season season'd are
To their right praise and true perfection ! —
Peace, ho ! the moon sleeps with Endymion,
And would not be awak'd.   [*Music ceases*]

LORENZO.   That is the voice,   110
Or I am much deceiv'd, of Portia.

PORTIA. He knows me, as the blind man knows the cuckoo,
By the bad voice.

LORENZO.   Dear lady, welcome home.

PORTIA. We have been praying for our husbands' welfare,
Which speed, we hope, the better for our words.   115
Are they return'd ?

109. **ho !** | hoa ! Malone | how
QqFf.
112, 113. As in Q2 | printed as
prose Ff.

114. **husbands'   welfare** | hus-
bands welfare Q2Ff | husband health
Q1 | husbands' healths Pope Camb.

106. The difference is in the hearer's mind, and not in the songs
themselves; and the nightingale is reputed the first of songsters
because she sings at the time when she can best be heard. We
have a like thought in *Sonnets*, CII.

107. A characteristic, if here somewhat unpleasant, jingle in 'season' and 'season'd.' The meaning is, that, by being rightly timed, the
things are tempered and made fit for their purpose ; hence relished.

109. Endymion was a very beautiful youth; Juno took a fancy
to him, whereupon Jupiter grew jealous, and cast him into a per-
petual sleep on Mount Latmos. While he was there asleep, Selene
(Luna), smitten with his beauty, used to come down and kiss him,
and lie by his side. According to one version, Selene herself put
him asleep, that she might have the pleasure of kissing him without
his knowledge. The story was naturally a favorite with the poets,
Lyly and Fletcher among the dramatists dealing with it, but young
Keats shaped the story into its most immortal poetic form.

LORENZO.   Madam, they are not yet;
But there is come a messenger before,
To signify their coming.

PORTIA.   Go in, Nerissa;
Give order to my servants that they take
No note at all of our being absent hence; —   120
Nor you, Lorenzo; — Jessica, nor you.   [*A tucket sounds*]

LORENZO. Your husband is at hand; I hear his trumpet:
We are no tell-tales, madam; fear you not.

PORTIA. This night methinks is but the daylight sick;
It looks a little paler: 't is a day,   125
Such as the day is when the sun is hid.

Enter BASSANIO, ANTONIO, GRATIANO, *and their followers*

BASSANIO. We should hold day with the Antipodes,
If you would walk in absence of the sun.

PORTIA. Let me give light, but let me not be light;
For a light wife doth make a heavy husband,   130
And never be Bassanio so for me:
But God sort all! You are welcome home, my lord.

BASSANIO. I thank you, madam. Give welcome to my
        friend:
This is the man, this is Antonio,
To whom I am so infinitely bound.   135

131. so for me QqF₁ | so from me F₂.

121. **tucket**: a peculiar series of notes on a trumpet. Probably
the word is from the Italian *toccata*. Cf. *Henry V*, IV, ii, 35.

127. **hold day with**: have day at the same time as.

129. Twice before in this play there has been punning upon the
word 'light.' Notice, too, the graceful play on 'bound' in l. 136.

132. **sort**: dispose. Cf. *Richard III*, II, iii, 36.

PORTIA. You should in all sense be much bound to him,
For, as I hear, he was much bound for you.

ANTONIO. No more than I am well acquitted of.

PORTIA. Sir, you are very welcome to our house :
It must appear in other ways than words,   140
Therefore I scant this breathing courtesy.

GRATIANO. [To NERISSA] By yonder moon I swear you
        do me wrong ;
In faith, I gave it to the judge's clerk.

PORTIA. A quarrel, ho, already! what's the matter?

GRATIANO. About a hoop of gold, a paltry ring   145
That she did give me ; whose poesy was
For all the world like cutler's poetry
Upon a knife, 'Love me, and leave me not.'

NERISSA. What talk you of the poesy or the value?
You swore to me, when I did give it you,   150
That you would wear it till your hour of death ;
And that it should lie with you in your grave :
Though not for me, yet for your vehement oaths,
You should have been respective, and have kept it.
Gave it a judge's clerk ! no, God's my judge,   155
The clerk will ne'er wear hair on 's face that had it.

---

146. poesy | poesie Q1Ff | posie Q2.   155. no, God 's my judge Qq |
151. your hour Qq | the hour Ff.   but wel I know Ff.

141. This complimentary form, made up only of breath, words.

146. poesy : the verse, or motto, inscribed in a ring. Usually
spelled in this sense 'posy.' As a motto ('sentiment') usually accom-
panied a gift of flowers, 'posy' came to mean a nosegay.

148. " Knives were formerly inscribed, by means of *aqua fortis*, with
short sentences in distich." — Sir John Hawkins, quoted by Reed.

154. respective : mindful, considerate. Cf. 'respect,' I, i, 74. Both
noun and adjective are used thus by Shakespeare.

GRATIANO.   He will, and if he live to be a man.

NERISSA.   Ay, if a woman live to be a man.

GRATIANO.   Now, by this hand, I gave it to a youth,
A kind of boy; a little scrubbed boy,   160
No higher than thyself, the judge's clerk;
A prating boy, that begg'd it as a fee:
I could not for my heart deny it him.

PORTIA.   You were to blame, I must be plain with you,
To part so slightly with your wife's first gift;   165
A thing stuck on with oaths upon your finger,
And so riveted with faith unto your flesh.
I gave my love a ring, and made him swear
Never to part with it; and here he stands:
I dare be sworn for him, he would not leave it,   170
Nor pluck it from his finger, for the wealth
That the world masters. Now, in faith, Gratiano,
You give your wife too unkind a cause of grief:
And 't were to me, I should be mad at it.   174

BASSANIO.   [Aside] Why, I were best to cut my left hand off,
And swear I lost the ring defending it.

GRATIANO.   My Lord Bassanio gave his ring away
Unto the judge that begg'd it, and indeed
Deserv'd it too; and then the boy, his clerk,
That took some pains in writing, he begg'd mine: 180
And neither man nor master would take aught
But the two rings.

160. **scrubbed**: stunted. From Anglo-Saxon *scrob*, 'shrub.' In
Holland's Pliny we have: "Such will never prove fair trees, but
scrubs only." And Verplanck observes that the name 'scrub oak'
was from the first settlement of America given to the dwarf or
bush oak. Warton suggested that Shakespeare wrote 'stubbed.'

PORTIA.   What ring gave you, my lord?
Not that, I hope, which you receiv'd of me.

BASSANIO. If I could add a lie unto a fault,
I would deny it; but you see my finger   185
Hath not the ring upon it, — it is gone.

PORTIA. Even so void is your false heart of truth.
By heaven, I will ne'er come in your bed
Until I see the ring.

NERISSA.   Nor I in yours
Till I again see mine.

BASSANIO.   Sweet Portia,   190
If you did know to whom I gave the ring,
If you did know for whom I gave the ring,
And would conceive for what I gave the ring,
And how unwillingly I left the ring,
When nought would be accepted but the ring,   195
You would abate the strength of your displeasure.

PORTIA. If you had known the virtue of the ring,
Or half her worthiness that gave the ring,
Or your own honour to contain the ring,
You would not then have parted with the ring.   200
What man is there so much unreasonable,
If you had pleas'd to have defended it
With any terms of zeal, wanted the modesty
To urge the thing held as a ceremony?
Nerissa teaches me what to believe :   205
I 'll die for 't but some woman had the ring.

199. contain : retain. It is used in the same sense in *Sonnets*,
LXXVII : "Look, what thy memory cannot contain." So in Bacon's
Essays, LVII, *Of Anger :* "To containe anger from mischiefe, though
it take hold of a man, there be two things."

BASSANIO. No, by mine honour, madam, by my soul,
No woman had it, but a civil doctor,
Which did refuse three thousand ducats of me,
And begg'd the ring; the which I did deny him,   210
And suffer'd him to go displeas'd away;
Even he that did uphold the very life
Of my dear friend. What should I say, sweet lady?
I was enforc'd to send it after him :
I was beset with shame and courtesy;   215
My honour would not let ingratitude
So much besmear it. Pardon me, good lady;
For, by these blessed candles of the night,
Had you been there, I think you would have begg'd
The ring of me to give the worthy doctor.   220

PORTIA. Let not that doctor e'er come near my house.
Since he hath got the jewel that I lov'd,
And that which you did swear to keep for me,
I will become as liberal as you;
I 'll not deny him any thing I have.   225

BASSANIO. Portia, forgive me this enforced wrong;

207. **mine** F_1F_2 | **my** Q_1Q_2.
211. **displeas'd away** Ff | **away**
displeas'd Q_1.

212. **did uphold** Q_1 | **had held up**
Q_2Ff.
218. **For** Qq | **And** Ff.

208. **civil doctor**: Doctor of Civil Law.

215. **shame and courtesy**: shame of discourtesy. Shakespeare
has several like expressions. In *King Lear*, I, ii, 48: "This policy
and reverence of age," meaning 'This policy, or custom, of rever-
encing age.' Also in *King Lear*, I, iv, 364: "This milky gentleness
and course of yours"; that is, 'milky and gentle course.' And
Hamlet, I, i, 87: "Well ratified by law and heraldry," meaning 'the
law of heraldry.'

218. The "candles of the night" are the moon and stars. So in
Romeo and Juliet, III, v, 9: "Night's candles are burnt out."

And, in the hearing of these many friends,
I swear to thee, even by thine own fair eyes,
Wherein I see myself, —

PORTIA.   Mark you but that !
In both my eyes he doubly sees himself;   230
In each eye, one : — swear by your double self,
And there 's an oath of credit.

BASSANIO.   Nay, but hear me :
Pardon this fault, and by my soul I swear
I never more will break an oath with thee.

ANTONIO.   I once did lend my body for his wealth ;   235
Which, but for him that had your husband's ring,
Had quite miscarried : I dare be bound again,
My soul upon the forfeit, that your lord
Will never more break faith advisedly.

PORTIA.   Then you shall be his surety. Give him this ; 240
And bid him keep it better than the other.

ANTONIO.   Here, Lord Bassanio ; swear to keep this ring.

BASSANIO.   By heaven, it is the same I gave the doctor !

PORTIA. I had it of him. You are all amaz'd :
Here is a letter ; read it at your leisure ;   245
It comes from Padua, from Bellario :
There you shall find that Portia was the doctor ;
Nerissa there her clerk : Lorenzo here
Shall witness I set forth as soon as you,

---

230. my F₁ | mine F₂.   235. his wealth Qq | thy wealth Ff.

235. For his welfare or his good. 'Wealth' is only another form
of 'weal': we say indifferently 'common-weal' or 'common-wealth';
and the 'commonwealth' is the good that men have in common.

236. **Which.** This refers to the loan of Antonio's body.

239. **advisedly**: deliberately. Cf. I, i, 142 ; II, i, 42.

And even but now return'd; I have not yet   250
Enter'd my house. — Antonio, you are welcome;
And I have better news in store for you
Than you expect: unseal this letter soon;
There you shall find three of your argosies
Are richly come to harbour suddenly: 255
You shall not know by what strange accident
I chanced on this letter.

ANTONIO.   I am dumb.

BASSANIO. Were you the doctor, and I knew you not?

ANTONIO. Sweet lady, you have given me life and living;
For here I read for certain that my ships   260
Are safely come to road.

PORTIA.   How now, Lorenzo!
My clerk hath some good comforts too for you.

NERISSA. Ay, and I 'll give them him without a fee. —
There do I give to you and Jessica,
From the rich Jew, a special deed of gift,   265
After his death, of all he dies possess'd of.

LORENZO. Fair ladies, you drop manna in the way
Of starved people.

PORTIA.   It is almost morning,
And yet I 'm sure you are not satisfied
Of these events at full. Let us go in;   270

---

250. even but Qq | but ev'n Ff.   270. Let us F1 | let's Q1.

251. In this welcome to Antonio and the announcement that his
argosies "with portly sail" (I, i, 9) are "richly come to harbour suddenly," Portia unravels the last tangle of the dramatic knot.

255. suddenly: unexpectedly. The First Folio spelling is 'sodainlie.'

259. Life and the means of living. Portia has given Antonio life
in delivering him from the clutches of Shylock.

And charge us there upon inter'gatories,
And we will answer all things faithfully.

   GRATIANO.   Let it be so : the first inter'gatory
That my Nerissa shall be sworn on is,
Whether till the next night she had rather stay,   275
Or go to bed now, being two hours to day :
Well, while I live I 'll fear no other thing
So sore as keeping safe Nerissa's ring.   *[Exeunt]*

   271. " In the Court of Queen's Bench, when a complaint is made
against a person for a ' contempt,' the practice is that, before sentence is finally pronounced, he is sent into the Crown Office, and,
being there ' charged upon interrogatories,' he is made to swear
that he will ' answer all things faithfully.' " — Lord Campbell.

INDEX

This Index includes the most important words, phrases, etc., explained in the notes. The figures in heavy-faced type refer to the pages; those in plain type, to the lines containing what is explained.